Coping With Dynamic Business Environments

This book discusses the existing management approaches for dealing with changes, namely readiness, maturity, and resilience. Although these concepts have been discussed for several years now, their importance grows when companies must deal with extended changes in economies. The changes are of a different nature: social, technological, and political, and they strongly impact every aspect of economies and companies' activity. Is it possible to be ready for the changes? Should companies be resilient to disruption? These are the questions the managers are trying to answer, yet they need some support from academics. This book explores the synergy between the state-of-the-art knowledge and experience of companies to create a Contemporary Management Model.

The scope of this book covers the methodology with an introduction and discussion of the key ideas and concludes with a presentation of the Contemporary Management Model followed by the practical validation and verification of the model based on case studies.

This book is simply about developing the readiness and resilience of resources and processes, especially from a tactical perspective.

Coping With Dynamic Business Environments

New Management Approaches for Resilience During Difficult Economies

Agnieszka Stachowiak

Routledge
Taylor & Francis Group

A PRODUCTIVITY PRESS BOOK

First published 2025
by Routledge
605 Third Avenue, New York, NY 10158

and by Routledge
4 Park Square, Milton Park, Abingdon, Oxon, OX14 4RN

Routledge is an imprint of the Taylor & Francis Group, an informa business

ISBN: 9781032688398 (hbk)
ISBN: 9781032688381 (pbk)
ISBN: 9781032688404 (ebk)

DOI: 10.4324/9781032688404

Typeset in Garamond
by codeMantra

Table of Contents

Acknowledgments

This book wouldn't have been possible without all the people who inspired my research and supported me along the way. I would like to thank my first supervisor, Professor Marek Fertsch, my colleagues from the Faculty of Engineering Management at PUT, and the colleagues from the International Board of Production Research. My special thanks go to Professor Shimon Nof, who introduced the topic of resilience to me, and Phd Eng Karolina Werner-Lewandowska, who shares my interest in the topic of maturity, not always sharing the same point of view, which makes our discussion creative.

This book could not be finalized without the continuous support of my family, their patience, and their belief in me. Thank you, Wojtek, Marta, Matylda, and Marcel.

There are many people who supported the book along the way. It takes a village to raise a child, and I think it takes a town to publish a book. Thank you all.

About the Author

Agnieszka Stachowiak studied at the Poznań University of Technology, majoring in Management and Marketing, specializing in Logistics. After completing her master's studies, she started doctoral studies, and in 2005, she obtained a doctoral degree. In the same year, she started working at the Poznań University of Technology. Her scientific interests include organizational resilience and maturity for agility and the implementation of modern solutions in production and logistics (Industry 4.0 and Logistics 4.0). Research in this area resulted in conferring the degree of habilitated doctor.

Agnieszka Stachowiak is the author and co-author of over 100 publications, including monographs and articles published in national and foreign journals, and presented at conferences around the world. She reviews scientific papers and has served as an assistant supervisor and supervisor in doctoral proceedings. She manages projects carried out by international consortia and performs research and design work for manufacturing and service companies.

She is involved in organizational activities at the university and beyond; she is the member of the board of the International Foundation for Production Research and a supporter of the Women in Production Research Forum. She is a member of the Polish Logistics Association, and she was an expert on the Future Industry Platform in Poland. She has co-organized a number of scientific conferences (including the Economy and Efficiency cyclical conference, ICPR – International Conference on Production Research, ICPR – AEM, InnoLog, and others) and is a member of the scientific committees of domestic and international conferences.

Since 2024, she has been the vice dean for science at the Faculty of Management Engineering at the Poznań University of Technology.

Introduction

Contemporary management faces numerous challenges. It needs to deal with geopolitical crises, environmental challenges, and economic disturbances. On the other hand, it can benefit from technological development, opportunities created by digitization, and globalization. There are both threats and opportunities, and organizations should be ready for them – to avoid threats, minimize their consequences, and identify opportunities that can be transformed into strengths and competitive advantage. The organization should also be mature to benefit from systemic and standardized management and resilient to thrive through the crises and dynamically recover.

This book explores the terms of readiness, maturity, and resilience and goes through exogenous and endogenous change drivers using a review of the literature. The review included available sources (open sources), and the selection was based on the impact criterion (the most cited sources) and the novelty criterion (the latest works).

Based on the conclusion from the literature review, the Management Excellence Model was developed, linking the methods and tools useful in contemporary business environments. The model was operationalized into a maturity model based on the assumption that flexible resources make organizations ready for change and resilient. Readiness and resilience together support an organization's maturity. Maturity is a construct that can be measured and the measure can be used to diagnose organizations, and the diagnosis can be transformed into recommendations for improvement. The example of diagnosis and the improvement recommendations are presented in the last section of this book.

This text can be used as an educational material, as it includes a review of the concepts important from a contemporary management perspective, and it can also be used as a guideline in business practice, as several models and methods of readiness, maturity, and resilience assessment are referred to; moreover, the integrated readiness, maturity, and resilience model is presented, explained, and implemented.

Introduction

Chapter 1

Shall Organizations Be Ready, Mature, or Resilient?

1.1 Readiness

1.1.1 Are You Ready?

1.1.1.1 Understanding the Term

Being ready means being prepared by having the necessary resources, both tangible and intangible, to deal with a specific situation or condition. Oxford (2010) indicates that readiness is "the state of being ready to do something". In a business context, readiness explains whether an organization is ready to start the development process or not (Akdil et al., 2018), or in a more general sense, "the state in which an organization is ready to perform a task" (Pacchini et al., 2019). Considering the above, readiness is a state that is achieved before starting a specific activity in relation to the psychological, behavioral, and structural aspects of the organization (Helfrich et al., 2011).

In literature, readiness is often related to changes and to the theory of an organization's readiness for change (or "readiness theory"), which can be treated as a contribution to the successful implementation of complex changes. The changes are of various ranges and natures, including technological changes (implementation of innovative technologies, e.g., in the areas of manufacturing and communication), adaptation to law regulations or expectations of stakeholders (e.g., SDG – Sustainable Development Goals and CSR – Corporate Social Responsibility), and strategic and structural changes. Since nowadays the pace of changes in technology as well as

DOI: 10.4324/9781032688404-1

the dynamics of economic and social changes are higher than before, the interest in readiness as a characteristics of organizations is growing, which is reflected in the growing number of publications on it. The concept of readiness is currently a topic of scientific research that is gaining increasing attention. This is evidenced by the growth rate of the number of publications related to readiness. The first publication on organizational readiness in the Scopus database dates back to 1987. There are several papers from the 1990s, but after the year 2000, the term became important for academics and business practitioners. Technological breakthroughs, inventions, innovations, but also crises: ecological, economical, and political induced changes in all aspects and areas of an organization's management. The changes result in the need for the new approaches, methods, and tools to deal with changes not only *post factum* but also *a priori* to them. To be ready for changes to come, organizational readiness for change refers to the involvement of organizational members in the change process, which determines the effective implementation of organizational change (Weiner et al., 2008, 2009). Such an approach focuses on a specific state of mental and behavioral preparation to adopt action (i.e., being willing and able to act) as a key aspect of organizational readiness for change (Weiner, 2009). Analysis of the available sources on organizational readiness (Scopus, search for organizational readiness, limited to business area, identified 372 sources) enables the development of the semantic map (presented in Figure 1.1, based on abstracts and keywords, and prepared with VosViewer), which, as assumed from the definitions and considerations presented, refers to mental and behavioral aspects, yet there are other aspects revealed as well.

The literature focuses on technical aspects, referring to technology adoption and solutions such as blockchain, cloud computing, IT systems, and e-commerce, service readiness, employees, linked to culture, participation, individual and group approach, change itself, and quality.

The clusters are interrelated, as readiness is a complex idea and should be considered from various perspectives. Hence, implementation of the TOE (Technology – Organization – Environment) context, which is an integrated approach to change understanding, as it is impossible to implement technology without changing organizations and having an impact on the environment, and at the same time, it is difficult to change organization or relations with the environment without implementing some technological solutions. As a result, the entire organization is involved. Early, yet most cited, works on organizational readiness refer to the implementation of solutions that are nowadays well recognized and often implemented. Iacovou et al. (1995) refer

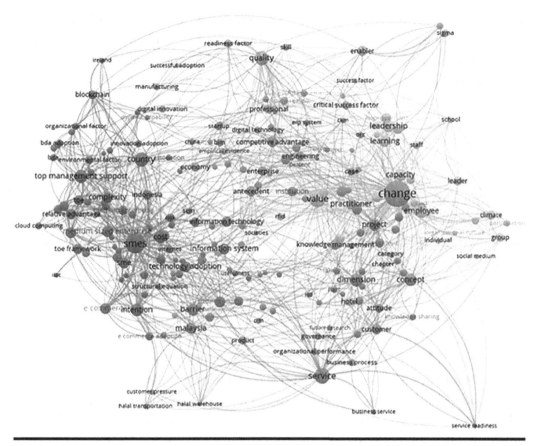

Figure 1.1 Readiness in literature: semantic map based on publications on readiness identified in the Scopus database (retrieved: December 1, 2023).

Source: Developed with VosViewer.

to EDI implementation in small companies. They identified a problem with EDI implementation in small companies and assumed that the reason for the problem was the resistance of small companies. To explore the problem, they conducted the research, including three factors influencing EDI implementation, namely: organizational readiness, external pressures to adopt, and perceived benefits. Though they relate these factors to small businesses only, they can be perceived as crucial for every business and the implementation of any solution (not only IT/technological). Based on the research results, Iacovou et al. developed a framework for EDI adoption by small businesses, and the value of the framework was confirmed by a multi-case study validation, while its universality was proven by the highest citation score.

Similar research was conducted by Mehrtens et al. (2001) in the context of Internet adoption/implementation. The same factors were recognized as significantly affecting Internet adoption: perceived benefits, organizational readiness, and external pressure. The subjects of the study were small companies as well, which made the results comparable and enabled identification of both similarities and differences between Internet adoption and EDI adoption in small companies.

Changes in technologies result in new challenges and solutions organizations have to be ready for. One of the solutions often analyzed in the context of readiness was electronic commerce. At the beginning of the 21st century, the opportunity to use electronic distribution channels was an opportunity to gain a competitive advantage, so it was intensively explored. Grandon and Pearson (2004) identified four factors influencing e-commerce adoption: organizational readiness, external pressure, perceived ease of use, and perceived usefulness. Their approach was based on TAM (Technology Acceptance Model), and some similarities to the previous approach presented can be identified, as the two first factors are identical, and the ease of use and perceived usefulness can be integrated into perceived benefits, yet not from the provider's perspective, but from the customer's perspective. The approach by Grandon and Pearson was also developed for small and medium companies, which leads to the conclusion that large enterprises are more ready thanks to the resources they have, and do need methodological support when preparing to take some actions or deal with a specific situation. They also experience less external pressures due to their size and competitive power. The conclusion, however, may not be legitimate when dealing with extremely complex actions and situations, as these may be demanding for large organizations as well.

Another challenge for companies was the implementation of advanced solutions, such as cloud computing. The approach presented by Gangwar et al. (2015) used perceived usefulness and perceived ease of use as mediating variables, which is a modification of previously presented approaches, while they identified relative advantage, compatibility, complexity, organizational readiness, top management commitment, and training and education as variables affecting cloud computing adoption. In their work internal conditions (created by top management commitment, training, and education) were recognized as important, and external pressure was not directly mentioned.

An analysis of organizational readiness can be conducted from an internal perspective to assess whether the company is ready to implement a change, but it can also be conducted from an external perspective to identify potential customers and recognize the market. Research by Ramdani et al. (2009) aimed to develop a model that can be used by software developers/

vendors to predict which companies are more likely to become adopters of enterprise systems (ERP, CRM, SCM, and e-procurement). In this case, the benefit of readiness assessment was the opportunity to create a marketing strategy for selling and promoting IT systems supporting enterprise management. The results proved that larger companies are more likely to implement such systems, which may result from the availability of resources but also from greater perceived relative advantage, greater experience with IT system implementation, greater top management support, and greater organizational readiness. As in the previous research presented in the chapter, technological and organizational factors were more important than environmental factors.

One step further is research on factors that facilitate or inhibit successful ERP implementation, as presented by Motwani et al. (2005). One of the factors identified is cultural readiness, accompanied by change management and network relationships. The conclusion from the research is that without organizational readiness and change management, ERP implementation is more likely to be unsuccessful, resulting in financial losses and worsening the overall situation of a company.

When referring to organizational factors, support from top management was mentioned in research by Ramdani et al. (2009) and Gangwar et al. (2015), whereas Eby et al. (2000) focused on individual attitudes and preferences, work groups, and job attitudes. The results of their research prove that they are important aspects of understanding readiness for change and developing strategies for organizational changes.

Understanding the changes and being ready to deal with them is a product of many variables, while technology-push and need-pull are often recognized as the driving forces. In the research by Lee and Shim (2007), they are accompanied by the presence of champions, which seems to be one of the aspects of top management support. Lee and Shim's research focused on adopting RFID, and their results prove that the likelihood of adopting RFID is strengthened or weakened by organizational readiness.

Contemporary companies are facing the technology-push phenomenon on an almost daily basis. The research by Clohessy and Acton (2019) deals with the organizational and environmental factors seeking to determine the impact of a developed (economically and technologically) environment on the implementation of blockchain, which is recognized as a disruptive innovation for many industries. The TOE approach used in the research enabled identification of patterns already recognized in the previously mentioned studies, namely: top management support and organizational readiness are enablers for blockchain adoption, and large companies are more likely to adopt blockchain than small to medium-sized enterprises (SMEs). The interesting conclusion, however, was that organizations that adopted blockchain used cloud-based blockchain platforms and tools to overcome the constraints of their initial low levels of organizational readiness. Hence, organizational readiness is an enabler but not necessarily a constraint when implementing changes, and it can be developed as a result of change implementation.

That conclusion is not commonly supported by the research results of other authors. Lokuge et al. (2019) suggest that the lack of organizational readiness is the reason for the failure of new products and services; hence, it is important to recognize the level of organizational readiness. They develop a multidimensional tool to measure organizational readiness with 21 measures, categorized under seven subconstructs: resource readiness, IT readiness, cognitive readiness, partnership readiness, innovation valance, cultural readiness, and strategic readiness. Their approach combines the knowledge of readiness and experience emerging from dealing with the challenges of the contemporary world.

The latest works on organizational readiness refer to the latest challenges companies are facing, coming from technology development, legal requirements, and economical, ecological, and political disturbances, but also strive for a better understanding of organizational readiness and its impact on companies.

The research by Najm and Ali (2024) aims to examine the effect of organizational readiness dimensions (organizational culture, climate, and capacity) on three types of innovations (service innovation, process innovation and entering new markets). The results indicate a positive effect of the two dimensions (climate and capacity) on process innovation and entering new markets. The deconstruction of organizational readiness enabled in-depth research and a better understanding of the phenomenon, and the conclusion that culture is not dynamic enough to support responding to changes and challenges is an original contribution to knowledge on organizational readiness. The authors conducted their research in the telecommunications sector, and they found the results specific due to the characteristics of this sector.

One of the technological and organizational challenges companies are dealing with nowadays is the successful implementation of the Industry 4.0 paradigm. The concept was coined in 2011 in Germany, and since that time, it has been the ambition of manufacturing companies to follow the guidelines defined to make manufacturing processes competitive on a global scale. The research by Samanta et al. (2024) identifies and analyzes critical success factors of the implementation of Industry 4.0 integrated with the lean six sigma approach. The critical success factors identified in the research include top management commitment, proving that the findings from the previous studies are still valid and accurate; organizational culture for adopting changes (which is different from the findings of Najm and Ali (2024), yet different sectors were analyzed in their case), organizational readiness, adaptability, and agility.

The research on Industry 4.0 implementation readiness was also conducted by Shahzad et al. (2023) with the well-established approach of analyzing organizational readiness together with relative advantage, compatibility, top management support, government regulation, and competitive pressure, in the TOE framework. Their results verified the importance of relative advantage, compatibility, competitive pressure, and top management support as enablers of Industry 4.0 implementation.

Confirmation of the previous results can also be found in another study by Shahzad et al. (2024). They focused on blockchain technology adoption and found that pre-adoption factors, including traceability, transparency, organizational readiness, coercive pressure, and normative pressure, positively influence blockchain technology adoption. The factors enlisted are similar to the ones identified by other researchers, not only for blockchain technology but also for other technologies as well, stressing organizational readiness and external pressures. The factor negatively affecting blockchain technology is security concerns, which were not mentioned before. However, a company's size as a factor differentiating organizational readiness was brought in before, and Shahzad et al. (2024) also recognized its impact on security concerns, finding that large organizations have higher readiness and lower security concerns than smaller companies.

The problem of blockchain technology adoption among small companies was also analyzed by Bag et al. (2023). They used the technology-organization-environment (TOE) framework and the resource-based view (RBV) perspective to find that relative advantage, compatibility, top management support, *organizational readiness*, competitive pressures, external support, regulations, and legislation significantly influence the implementation of blockchain technology in small and medium companies, whereas top management support is the most critical predictor of blockchain technology adoption, followed by organizational readiness and competitive pressures. The study was conducted in the developing countries, comparing its results with the research conducted in developed country example (Clohessy and Acton, 2019).

The context of readiness that is comparatively new is sustainability. Even though the sustainability concept has been present in literature, legal frameworks, and business practice since 1991 (Brundtland report publication), previous research on readiness did not pay much attention to it.

However, since companies face penalties or are barred from exporting for not meeting the regulations and standards for sustainability they should be ready to implement them and embrace environmentally oriented changes as well. The research by Ullah et al. (2024) proves that their original Organizational Readiness for Green Innovation (ORGI) approach has a direct positive effect on sustainability performance. The factors stressed in the context of organizational readiness were green innovation and knowledge integration, covering both organizational aspects of internal readiness and environmental aspects of the legal (instead of technology) push.

Sustainable development goals are a challenge for many companies, and Haritas and Das (2023) in their research identify current challenges in the firm-level implementation of the SDGs. They stress the importance of over-all *organizational readiness* to seize business opportunities and help pursue a course of action toward true sustainability. The result of their research is a goal-oriented transformative approach that enables businesses to develop their roadmaps for achieving business sustainability and supporting the realization of the SDGs. In this context, organizational readiness is crucial for doable goal definition and implementation within the framework of the SDGs.

Another context of readiness not analyzed before is the context of the supply chain. Shifting from a single company's perspective to a supply chain perspective makes organizational readiness more complex and multi-dimensional since contemporary supply chains operate in a strong institutional environment that influences various aspects like technology adoption and digitalization. The research by Tiwari et al. (2024) explores the topic of digitalization in the supply chain and presents a model to investigate digitalization readiness. The research does not refer to any specific digital technology, which makes the model universal. The conclusion presented is that organizational readiness and people readiness are critical elements of digitalization readiness, which confirms previous research by other authors conducted for single organizations. Changing perspectives on the supply chain does not change the concept of readiness, nor does the industry. The research conducted by Hassan et al. (2023) on logistics (cold chain services) proved again that top management support and *organizational readiness* were the key factors influencing the intention to implement change in cold chain logistics services.

Organizational readiness enables change implementation, and, according to the research results by Bilgiç et al. (2023), changes such as successful digital transformation help in learning and gaining resilience. Bilgiç et al. found that adaptive and data-driven cultures support flexibility, innovation, and decision-making processes and concluded that culture embracing adaptability, communication, ethics, and sustainability is the key to navigate digitalization and achieve sustainable growth.

Ethical concerns are presented when considering the adoption of generative artificial intelligence, as it has a continuously growing impact on many areas of humans' lives. Even though the latest technology is analyzed, the generic technology-organization-environment (TOE) framework is implemented in the research by Al-Khatib (2023). The results indicate that relative advantage, top management support, organizational readiness, and customer pressures positively influence GEN-AI adoption, whereas the influence of compatibility and competitive pressures on GEN-AI adoption is insignificant. Analysis of the research results presented in the literature proves that the factors positively influencing change adaptation do not differ on account of technology, which makes readiness a general and universal concept.

1.1.2 Measuring and Assessing Readiness

To know whether a company is ready, it needs tools to measure and assess its readiness. Readiness assessment includes the analysis and determination of the level of preparation, attitudes, and resources at all levels of the system (Mittal et al., 2018), as readiness can be observed at many levels and then analyzed individually, at the team, department, or organization level (Molla, 2009). However, one aspect of this difficulty arises from the fact that the concept of "readiness" only has full meaning in the context of: "ready for what?" (Tetlay and John, 2009). Hence, "metrics" such as "Technology Readiness Levels" (TRL) (e.g. Mankins, 1995) "System Readiness Levels" (SRL) "Integration Readiness Levels" (IRL) (e.g. Gove et al., 2008) "Manufacturing Readiness Levels" (MRL), and many others were developed. Their practical implementation differs on account of the quality of the measure description and the possibility of referring the assessment model presented in a specific case to other cases. Research (Sauser et al., 2008) revealed the difficulty of achieving meaningful, clear and measurable indicators.

According to Dowling and Pardoe, "readiness" values are typically soft measures that are relatively easy to calculate but require supporting justification that explains the assessment, are human-intensive, subjective, contain inherent differences or ambiguities that are averaged out (Dowling and Pardoe, 2005).

Yet, since there are numerous publications on readiness models and readiness assessment, some of the approaches will be presented in the following sections to contribute to a better understanding of the concepts presented in the second chapter.

1.1.2.1 Technology Readiness Level (TRL)

The basic readiness scale to be introduced is the Technology Readiness Level. The scale does not refer to organizational readiness and is often linked with maturity assessment.

The concept was introduced by NASA in 1974, developed over the next few years, and defined formally in 1989. It was supposed to support decisions aimed at risk mitigation and measuring the progress of a project.

Though initially dedicated for military purposes (used by NASA, DoD (Department of Defence), and ESA (European Space Agency)), it was adopted by the European Commission in 2010 and advised for implementation by EU-funded research and innovation projects. In 2013, TRL was formally presented in the ISO 16290:2013 standard by the International Organization for Standardization (ISO). Since 2014, the Technology Readiness Level scale has been consequently used in the EU Horizon 2020 program. The widely and universally adopted scale includes nine levels of technology readiness described as follows (based on NATO and EU principles):

TRL1: (basic principles observed (and reported), the lowest level of technology readiness) – At this stage, scientific research begins to be translated into applied research and development. Examples might include paper studies of a technology's basic properties.

TRL2: (Technology concept and/or application formulated; at this stage, invention process begins) – Once basic principles are observed, practical applications can be invented. Applications are speculative, and there may be no proof or detailed analysis to support the assumptions. Examples are limited to analytic studies.

TRL3: (Analytical and experimental critical function and/or characteristic proof of concept) – At this stage, active research and development are initiated. This includes analytical studies and laboratory studies to physically validate analytical predictions of separate elements of the technology. Examples include components that are not yet integrated or representative.

TRL4: (Component and/or breadboard technology validation in a laboratory environment) – At this stage, basic technological components are integrated to establish that they will work together. This is relatively "low fidelity" compared to the eventual system. Examples include the integration of "ad hoc" hardware in the laboratory.

TRL5: (Component and/or breadboard validation in relevant environment) – Technology validated in relevant environment (industrially relevant environment in the case of key enabling technologies). At this stage, the fidelity of breadboard technology increases significantly. The basic technological components are integrated with reasonably realistic supporting elements so they can be tested in a simulated environment.

TRL6: (System/subsystem model or prototype demonstration in a relevant environment (ground or space) – Technology demonstrated in relevant environment (an industrially relevant environment in the case of key enabling technologies). At this stage, a representative model or prototype system, which is well beyond that of TRL 5, is tested in a relevant environment. Represents a major step up in a technology's demonstrated readiness.

TRL7: (System prototype demonstration in an operational environment) – System prototype demonstration in an operational environment. At this stage, the prototype is near, or at, the planned operational system. Represents a major step up from TRL 6, requiring the demonstration of an actual system prototype in an operational environment such as an aircraft, vehicle, or space.

TRL8: (Actual system completed and qualified through test and demonstration) – The system is complete and qualified. At this stage, technology has been proven to work in its final form and under expected conditions. In almost all cases, this TRL represents the end of true system development. Examples include developmental tests and evaluations of the system in its intended weapon system to determine whether it meets design specifications.

TRL9: (Actual system has proven through successful mission) – Actual system proven in operational environment (competitive manufacturing in the case of key enabling technologies; or in space) operations. The actual application of the technology in its final form and under mission conditions, such as those encountered in operational testing and evaluation. Examples include using the system under operational mission conditions.

The Technology Readiness Levels can be implemented to measure the maturity of a given technology (a product or its components). The result of measurement gives a clear answer on what stages of product development are finished and what needs to be completed before the product is ready to be used, hence it measures the progress of a product development project (https://acqnotes.com/references, Technology Readiness Assessment (TRA) Deskbook by DoD).

1.1.2.2 Organizational Readiness for Digital Innovation

One of the contexts of readiness presented in the discussion on organizational readiness in literature is digitization. The approach presented aims to be universal, without indicating any specific digital technology. The elements (subconstructs) of overall Organizational Readiness for Digital Innovation were identified based on the literature analysis and presented in the paper by Lokuge et al. (2019). The subconstructs include:

Resource readiness – in the context of resources (technical resources/technology, human resources, and financial resources) their flexibility is crucial. A company is ready for change (digitalization) if it can configure and reconfigure its resources, and recognizes the opportunities emerging from shred resource use. Flexibility is easier in small and medium companies as large companies are usually more structured and hierarchical; however, the availability of resources and the potential of acquiring resources are usually greater in big companies.

Cultural readiness – the aspect of culture is specific as it refers to the core values of an organization and in the context of digital innovation implementation the core values should be focused on innovation appreciation. The organization should be open to new concepts and ideas, use decentralized decision-making to dedicate solutions to selected areas and problems, and have low-risk aversion. Nowadays, organizations employing people who are digital natives use the latest technological solutions, which increases their openness to innovation and acceptance of change.

Strategic readiness – top management support is crucial for digital innovation and this support is manifested by developing and presenting a plan of action and defined guidelines for compliance with innovation. Managers are responsible for clarity of plans, continuous refinement, and open communication while presenting strategic goals.

IT readiness – in the context of IT, stability of IT systems, security of data, and accessibility of solutions such as clouds, wearables, mobile, social media, and business analytics are important. Accessibility these days is enabled by subscriptions offered by IT providers, enabling easy on-demand access to selected solutions. Security is a growing concern for many companies, and cybersecurity providing solutions are sought and implemented to ensure, among other stability of enterprise systems.

Innovation valance – the decision to implement digital innovation impacts the entire organization and its environment; hence, the support of all the stakeholders is crucial. The support manifests itself in the general positive attitude of employees toward digital innovation, motivation, and empowerment. These aspects are especially important when the implementation of the digital innovation process is disturbed by a lack of resources.

Cognitive readiness – cognitive readiness is knowledge oriented and focused on knowledge, skills and adaptability of staff. The most important areas of knowledge are business processes and software, while the skills should cover technical skills. Adaptability is mostly about learning and adapting to new situations/challenges. Continuous learning and development of knowledge is crucial in knowledge-based societies and organizations, due to the growth of knowledge and the development of new technologies.

Partnership readiness – the key aspect is the will and ability to initiate and maintain relationships with various stakeholders, including suppliers, consultants, software and hardware providers, and consultants. The need to cooperate is on the one hand resulting from the specifics of digitization and the expertise required to implement digital innovations, and on the other the long-term trend of creating supply chains operating in global conditions.

In the model by Lokuge et al. (2019), the subcontracts are deconstructed into specific statements. Relating to the statements enables the mapping of partial and overall readiness. The statements constitute the assessment tool, which takes the form of a digital innovation readiness survey instrument.

The survey starts with a brief intro: "This survey measures the readiness of your organization to innovate with digital technologies" (Lokuge et al., 2019). The term IT portfolio in the survey refers to technologies like cloud computing, wearables, mobile technologies, social media, and business analytics. In this survey, the term innovation refers to "the production or adoption, assimilation, and exploitation of a value-added novelty in economic and social spheres; renewal and enlargement of products, services, and markets; development of new methods of production; and establishment of new management systems" (Lokuge et al., 2019), which is followed by statements organized into subconstructs:

Resource readiness:

> (R-1) My organization is flexible in allocating adequate financial resources necessary to innovate with the IT portfolio.
> (R-2) My organization is flexible in allocating adequate human resources necessary to innovate with the IT portfolio.
> (R-3) My organization is flexible in allocating adequate IT infrastructure resources necessary to innovate with the IT portfolio.

Cultural readiness:

> (C-1) My organization has a well-established way of sharing ideas and thoughts to engage with the IT portfolio for innovations.
> (C-2) My organization has a decentralized decision-making process that facilitates the engagement of all business areas to use the IT portfolio for innovations.
> (C-3) My organization takes reasonable risk assessment of engaging IT to facilitate innovations.

Strategic readiness:

(S-1) Our organizational strategic goals are clear to me when engaging the IT portfolio to facilitate innovations.

(S-2) Our organizational strategic goals are relevant to me when using the IT portfolio to facilitate innovations.

(S-3) I am well-aware of our organizational strategic goals communicated to me for using the IT portfolio to facilitate innovations.

IT readiness:

(T-1) Enterprise system/s in my organization is/are stable, up-to-date, and reliable.

(T-2) I have access to a range of new technologies like cloud, mobile, social media, and big data analytics available to facilitate innovations.

(T-3) Our IT infrastructure is stable, up-to-date, and reliable to facilitate innovations.

Innovation valance:

(Iv-1) Our staff members have the right attitudes that facilitate innovations.

(Iv-2) Our staff members are motivated to facilitate innovations.

(Iv-3) Our staff members are empowered to make decisions that facilitate innovations.

Cognitive readiness:

(Cg-1) Our staff members have the appropriate knowledge (i.e., technical, business process, and organizational) to facilitate innovations.

(Cg-2) Our staff members have the appropriate skills to facilitate innovations.

(Cg-3) Our staff members have the appropriate adaptability to facilitate innovation.

Partnership readiness:

(Pr-1) My organization has a good relationship with the software vendors to facilitate innovations.

(Pr-2) My organization has a good relationship with the management consultants to facilitate innovations.
(Pr-3) My organization has a good relationship with our suppliers and vendors to facilitate innovations.

Additionally, there are global measures of organizational readiness for digital innovation:

(Global-1) Our IT portfolio is well-equipped to support any innovations in the organization.
(Global-2) Our organization is well-equipped to support any innovations.

Supported by innovation implementation effectiveness:

(InnovationImp-1) We are good at implementing new ideas in the organization.
(InnovationImp-2) We have introduced enough new products and services to compete with our competition.
(InnovationImp-3) Most of our new ideas are now implemented.

Conducting such assessments in a company requires collecting opinions from many sources to confront and contrast various points of view and perspectives. A readiness assessment based on a single opinion may be compromised by a lack of knowledge in a specific field or a lack of understanding of a specific problem. The opinions collected should be statistically processed, and the approach by Lokuge et al. (2019) can be used.

1.1.2.3 Industry 4.0 Readiness Model

Industry 4.0 encompasses digitization, however the concept is larger and encompasses various solutions. The Industry 4.0 readiness model developed by Nick et al. (2021) is based on the Intervention Points. These points are grouped in dimensions such as Physical world, Virtual world, Human, Products and services, Value chain, Environment and Strategy, and Culture.

Physical world dimension is related to the Industry 4.0 term – Cyber-Physical System (CPS) and includes: autonomous operation, upgradeability of production equipment and infrastructure, data acquisition, information exchange and communication, and state-of-the-art technologies. Intervention points connected with the physical world dimension are focused on technical equipment, used in manufacturing processes, technologies supporting production, and logistics processes.

Virtual world dimension is related to the Industry 4.0 term – digital twin, and includes: data acquisition and storage, data exploitation, digital twins, automated, intelligent processes, and security awareness of the company. Intervention points connected with the virtual world are focused on IT solutions implemented to support manufacturing and management processes, including decision making and providing security of data (confidentiality and integrity) and of processes (compliance with regulatory requirements).

Human dimension is related to the role of people in a new business model. This dimension is related not only to Industry 4.0 but also to Industry 5.0, which adds human perspective to technology oriented Industry 4.0. The human dimension includes the role of people in manufacturing, openness to new technologies, internal training for new technologies, a digital workplace, and a safe working environment. Intervention points connected with the human dimension are focused on the new roles that people in Industry 4.0 need to take and the skills and attitudes they need to have to benefit from new technologies and to develop and improve them.

Products and services dimension is related to the structure of products and processes and seeks to determine the level of digitalization understanding. This dimension includes the digitalization of products, data about the product, utilization of data, understanding customer needs, and environmental awareness. Intervention points connected with the products and services dimension are focused on new innovative products that are developed to meet customer needs and follow requirements connected with sustainability and environmental impact.

Value chain dimension is connected with processes linked and integrated to create value for products, and moreover, to integrate companies into supply chains and networks of international/global range. The value chain dimension includes digital partner connections, strong partnerships, research and innovative networks, prominent role in the value chain, and a sustainable supply chain. Intervention points connected with the value chain focus on integration that can be achieved through the use of digital data, communication, and knowledge sharing.

Environment dimension is connected with competitiveness and sustainability and follows the sustainable development concept of balancing financial/economic, social, and environmental resources. It includes: infrastructure, regulatory environment, financial resources, labor-force, and cooperation opportunities. Intervention points connected with the environment are focused on assessing whether the environment supports the implementation of changes and the adoption of Industry 4.0, offering access to infrastructure, financial resources, and human resources, and enabling compliance with legal regulations.

Strategy and culture – dimension is connected with links between strategy and the Industry 4.0 concept and includes: HR strategy, Industry 4.0 strategy, strategy implementation, research, development, and innovation, and company culture. Intervention points are focused on assessing the level of incorporating Industry 4.0 elements into the company's strategy and building a culture that embraces and appreciates elements of Industry 4.0.

The model presented can be used for Industry 4.0 readiness assessment. Intervention points allow a company to recognize its strong and weak points and identify gaps to be filled in by managerial efforts to make the company more ready for Industry 4.0 adoption.

The assessment is subjective; hence, as in the previous model presented, it requires collecting opinions from many sources to confront and contrast various points of view and perspectives. A readiness assessment based on a single opinion may be compromised by a lack of knowledge in a specific field or a lack of understanding of a specific problem. The opinions collected should be statistically processed to conclude on the partial (dimension-wise) and overall level of Industry 4.0 readiness.

1.1.2.4 Sustainability Readiness Model

The sustainability readiness model selected for presentation has a structure typical for maturity model. It was presented by Barlett et al. (2021) and developed on the basis of a literature review and my own research. The model comprises of four readiness levels referred to as scores, namely:

Score 0: organization unprepared – Zero level of readiness means that the organization is not ready to build in sustainability into its manufacturing and management systems.

Score 1: novice – Novice level of readiness means that the organization is learning to build sustainability into its manufacturing and management systems.

Score 2: almost ready but static – This level of readiness means that the organization knows how to build sustainability into its manufacturing and management systems and it already has. However, no development or improvement efforts were made.

Score 3: ready, continuous improver – This level of readiness means that the organization successfully built in sustainability into its manufacturing and management systems, moreover, it strives for continuous improvement in the field.

Manufacturing and management systems areas that are examined in the context of readiness are: manufacturing processes, assets, materials, data driven decision support, information systems, and organizational competences.

Readiness assessment based on the model by Barlett et al. (2021) exploits various methods and tools of data collection that include: observations at the production facility, in-depth interviews and focus-group interviews.

The data was collected to recognize the ability of capturing and unifying knowledge of transformation processes, as well as of monitoring and controlling product and production performance. These aspects are important from the sustainability of manufacturing processes perspective as they prove that the company is aware of the impact of production on the natural environment. Another aspect analyzed was the methods of securing the quality of materials and consumables, securing efficiency in the use of materials and consumables, and securing the quality and efficiency of production equipment. These aspects are important from a resources perspective – sustainability assumes rational natural resource management, including materials and consumables use and waste generation, hence the analysis of the aspect of efficiency.

The approach to collecting, storing, managing and using "appropriate" data infrastructure was also analyzed to inform on data availability and format.

In the context of information and communication technologies (ICT) and analytic tools governance, the methods used for enabling quantitative and statistical analysis for/in product lifecycle management and the production system's management were the subject of analysis. Lifecycle management is crucial for sustainability because it gives a holistic understanding of a product's impact on the environment. Human resources were also analyzed, especially in the context of methods of incentivizing employees and defining clear roles and responsibilities for employees. The human resources aspect is a crucial component of sustainability (composed of social, economic, and environmental issues).

Specific aspects of human resources are competences, and the methods of capturing, storing, and maintaining relevant knowledge on a shared platform were identified. Knowledge resources are an important aspect of readiness as they affect the production system's economic and environmental performance positively and identify its impact on the environment and society. Consequently, identification of an approach to developing relevant organizational competences is also crucial for recognizing organizational readiness to change (sustainability principles/goals adoption).

Data collected in the areas listed above with the methods used by Barlett et al. (2021) in their model enables sustainability readiness assessment. The analysis was qualitative and based on coding in two dimensions, namely the categories (explained) and readiness levels. The results of the assessment are easily understandable and can be practically used; the identification of gaps (areas with low readiness levels) can be improved to increase the overall readiness of the company.

1.1.2.5 Online Readiness Assessment

Online assessment is available, fast, and convenient. This is why there are numerous online tools offered to conduct assessments in various fields.

An example of readiness assessment is the one offered by UML (https://www.uml.edu/research/cph-new/healthy-work-participatory-program/get-ready/assess-readiness/readiness.aspx). The tool aims to assess an organization's existing knowledge and competencies in health, safety, and wellness. Suggestions are provided on how to integrate these existing competencies into the Healthy Workplace Participatory Program (HWPP). The readiness assessment is a two-stage procedure. The first stage is the 7-item online survey as a quick screen to assess the organization's readiness for the HWPP. After the assessment, feedback is given and extra materials are offered to learn more about the concept and increase readiness). Next, the 24-item Organizational Readiness Survey is conducted, for a thorough evaluation of the resources available to implement the HWPP. Hence, the assessment is dedicated to recognize specific capabilities.

Another example of an online readiness assessment is the Digital Readiness Assessment (DRA) (https://digitalreadiness.ey.com/). The assessment is also a benchmarking tool. It provides assessments and benchmarks digital maturity across seven focus areas:

- Strategy, Innovation, and Growth
- Customer Experience
- Supply Chain and Operations
- Technology
- Risk and Cyber Security
- Finance, Legal, and Tax
- People and Organization

Performance in each area is assessed, showing the organization's current ability to navigate the digital world and presenting ideas for adjusting its business strategy to mitigate the risk of digital disconnection and seize opportunity with digital investment.

Expected benefits from assessment include:

- Identification of digital strengths, weaknesses, and gaps
- Benchmarking by sector, geography, or business size. Comparing with competitors in the same sector – and against digital leaders in other sectors.
- Exploring differing views by business function or see how other business leaders seeing their digital readiness

Digital readiness can also be assessed with the tool offered by Digilab Finance (International Finance Corporation, in cooperation with the World Bank Group) (https://digilabfinance.org/survey/self-assessment-tool). The tool is free and available online, It was introduced with simple instructions. It can be implemented to assess the digital readiness of an organization via the self-assessment of the organization's members. The diagnosis allows for the development of a new digital strategy and a digital transformation roadmap. The first step of the assessment is understanding the state/level of digital maturity of an organization to identify the starting point of the digital transformation process. The results of this step will be used throughout the process of increasing the digital readiness of an organization.

1.1.3 Conclusion

Readiness is a general and universal term and a measure often implemented in various areas, just to mention psychology (e.g., school readiness) and engineering (e.g., TRL – Technology Readiness Level). From a management perspective, readiness is considered in the context of changes. Companies nowadays are strongly exposed to changes of various natures: legislative, technological, political, and economical, resulting from local and global disruption and emerging trends. The changes can be a threat or a chance, depending on the organization's attitude and the resources available. Hence, building readiness seems to be crucial, and both the human perspective (focused on change recognition and acceptance), and the technical resources perspective (focused on flexibility and universality of technical resources) should be implemented. Organizational readiness is quite specific as organizations are complex systems composed of various resources and processes, the readiness of which synergistically contributes to overall performance. However, low readiness in one of the areas can substantially decrease the ability to embrace change and incorporate it into an organization's routines.

1.2 Maturity

1.2.1 Could You Be More Mature?

1.2.1.1 Understanding the Term

Lots of people have heard the question and need to rethink their attitude. The term "maturity" is used in many contexts, in everyday situations, and is usually positive; a mature person is someone who is fully developed in biological, psychological, and emotional terms. It is someone who is responsible, reliable, and predictable. The term is used in biology, where a "mature organism is one that has completely grown and developed for any function or state (..) the state of full development or completed growth is referred to as maturity" (https://www.biologyonline.com/dictionary/maturation).

In psychology maturity is defined as the level of psychological functioning one can attain, after which the level of psychological functioning no longer increases much with age (Wechsler, 1950).

The term "maturity" is a term used colloquially and intuitively: "mature" is one who has achieved a certain level of knowledge, understanding, wisdom and responsibility, therefore it is a combination of features that together, synergistically, testify about the object. Basically, maturity is associated with a social value that has a positive connotation (Zymonik and Fiałkowska, 2013). A typical way of colloquially defining maturity is to define it as a normatively postulated and axiologically valuable way of behaving or a set of features (depending on the object of reference). Maturity includes phenomena that may be subject to change or development, and the process of achieving maturity is related to improving skills and achieving certain features, and also means readiness for specific tasks (Sajdak, 2010). The process of achieving maturity is related to the passage of time. However, time is not the only determinant. A specific set of conditions is also required, thanks to which the achievement of maturity is possible and for this reason, the issue is undertaken and research of a theoretical and applied nature is developed, which has been observed since the 1970s in various areas of the organization's activity (Dobrowolska, 2013). Therefore, organizational maturity, like human maturity, is a complex concept, but due to the research conducted in the field of maturity, it already has a developed generic typology and a typology of images that highlight different approaches to maturity. From a substantive point of view, it is important that the emphasized complexity of maturity does not mean that it is an ambiguous concept (Kuc, 1999). The already mentioned basic, intuitive interpretation of this term is widely accepted, especially its reference to universal categories of development. On the basis of development theory, differentiation is made by creating terminological explanations of maturity, taking into account the specific nature of the examined object.

Both angles present maturity as a state of full development and growth, reaching the maximal capabilities of an organism. The term well recognized and widely used was transferred to the field of management in the 80s of the 20th century. The first publication on organizational maturity available in Scopus was by Benbasat et al. (1980), and the number of publications (hence, interest and research) started to grow in the 90s. The introduction of the terms and literature on maturity presented in the chapter is based on an analysis of 97 papers on organizational maturity indexed in the Scopus database in the field of business and management. The most cited and latest publications were analyzed in the greatest detail to reflect the most recognized and contemporary approaches used in organizational maturity studies (Figure 1.2).

The literature focuses on change, referring to strategy and the manager's role, organizational culture, process approach, practical use of the maturity approach, and analysis and assessment of maturity level.

In the definitions, most authors refer to the expected target state – mature organisms reach the highest level of development, and it is the same with organizations – to be mature, they need to achieve a certain level of performance. The key issue in defining organizational maturity is deciding what the expected target level of performance is, and there are various approaches presented. The first area where the concept of organization maturity was planted in the early 1990s was the software development industry (and the early maturity models are software development oriented). The originality of the approach was based on the assumption that software quality depends on organizational and management styles and that software engineering can be a more effective method of turning chaotic software development into a more controlled and manageable process (Humphrey, 1989).

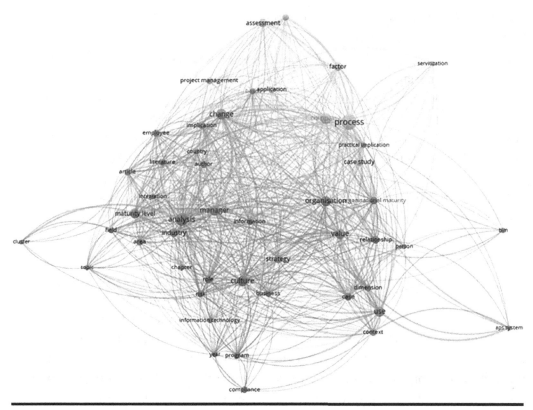

Figure 1.2 Maturity in literature: semantic map based on publication identified in the Scopus database (retrieved: December 1, 2023).

Source: Developed with VosViewer.

Software development processes were the key area for addressing organizational maturity and identifying stages or levels of maturity: from an initial level to a repeatable, defined, managed, and an optimizing level. The levels are defined to describe maturing, the evolution from ad hoc, chaotic processes to mature, disciplined software processes, and the degree to which a process is institutionalized and effective (Paulk et al., 1993).

With time, the definition and implementation of the organizational maturity concept have become more universal and area- neutral. Software development was not directly addressed, and the following dimensions were recognized: (1) standardization, which is concerned with process and product standardization in the organization, (2) project management, which is concerned with the extent to which good project management practices are employed, (3) tools, which is concerned with effective automated tool usage in the organization, and (4) organization, which is concerned mainly with the alignment of the IS organization with the overall business (El Emam and Madhavji, 1995).

Efficiency of organizations is stressed in many maturity definitions, including the ones by (Skrzypek, 2014), where she emphasizes that the maturity of an organization is primarily associated with a high level of various forms of management efficiency (efficiency, effectiveness).

Another approach to maturity definition is to focus on progress and development. Resemann and de Bruin in their research (Resemann and de Bruin, 2005) present a general and universal explanation of maturity as the ability to develop the capabilities of a given organization in the area of its operation.

Development is naturally connected with striving for improvement and striving for excellence. To start with, striving for excellence through continuous improvement and growth was consistent with the biological approach to maturity. The same concept was used in an organizational context by Hammer, linking improvement with efficiency. He defines maturity as the systematic improvement of the organization's skills and processes in order to achieve higher efficiency in a given period of time (Hammer, 2007). In his opinion, maturity is the improvement of both the organization's skills and the processes implemented in it, in order to achieve higher efficiency in a given period of time. He emphasizes that the organization should strive to acquire maturity on a continuous basis, and systematicity in activities undertaken as part of the continuous improvement process is necessary (Hammer, 2007).

When striving for excellence, one still needs to be aware of limitations and constraints. Michael Porter defines the maturity of an organization as being aware of its limitations and willing to eliminate them. Porter points out the need to maintain flexibility and constantly strive to transfer good practices in the strategic and operational spheres. He also emphasizes that the operational sphere is an area that allows for the introduction of changes, concern for flexibility and tireless efforts to use proven, exemplary practices (Porter, 2005).

Maturity is a target state, therefore one that should be strived for by actively developing and improving. Seeking maturity, an organization should improve the configuration of its resources (social and technical), the effectiveness and efficiency of implemented processes, and its relations with the environment. This is a demanding task because resources, the environment, and expectations regarding processes are variable. The endogenous and exogenous constraints of the organization are also subject to change. As a result, striving for maturity requires a conscious, flexible response to the changing environment, agility (Stachowiak, 2019), and following the path of continuous improvement – although progress in achieving maturity is usually perceived not as continuous (evolutionary), but in leaps (revolutionary), expressed through subsequent levels of maturity.

The issue of maturity is related to the ability to change and develop, and the process of achieving maturity is related to improving skills and acquiring certain features. The manifestations of maturity include efficiency, effectiveness, productivity, and efficiency (Skrzypek, 2014). According to the definition, maturity is the systematic improvement of the organization's skills, as well as the processes implemented in it, in order to achieve higher efficiency in a given period of time (Kłos, 2013).

Since maturity is usually defined in terms of development theory (Borys, 2013), its changeable and evolutionary nature is indicated. Maturity is achieved gradually. Therefore, we can talk about maturity gradations and, consequently, about maturity levels, which are understood as the degree of development of an object (Kosieradzka, 2016).

The level of maturity will be the degree to which the positive/desirable features of an object are realized, revealed in the form of maturity symptoms such as perfection, responsibility, wisdom, intelligence, and others (Borys, 2013). This approach enables the standardization of maturity assessment and the development of reference models for improvement, i.e., the ability of the organization, including its processes, to systematically improve the results delivered as part of its activities (Kalinowski, 2012). Maturity can be interpreted in a synthetic way (holistic, integrated maturity, revealed in the concept of a perfect and sustainable organization) or by decomposition at the facility level (management, process, quality, cultural maturity) or at the praxeological level (maturity in effectiveness, efficiency, efficiency). Maturity manifests itself in various dimensions, e.g., social, economic, biological, market, and technical (Skrzypek, 2014). The approach to maturity based on decomposition is called specialized.

In the context of maturity gradation, which can also be applied to organizations, it can be assumed that specialized maturity, achieved in some/selected aspects of functioning or elements of the organization, is a lower level, and integrated, holistic maturity is a higher level of maturity. Therefore, enterprises should strive to synthesize decomposed maturities, and even in addition to internal integration, they should also strive for external integration, because paths based on the destruction of maturity, and, in the axiological sense, on the egocentric trend, reveal the characteristics of an immature object (Borys, 2013).

Integrated maturity refers to the entire organization, and from this perspective, we talk about an excellent or resilient organization.

Improvement and excellence from a practical perspective are often associated with standardization and repeatability. For example, according to SEI

(Software Engineering Institute), maturity is the degree of an organization's ability to repeat production processes as well as operational and strategic management. From a quality management perspective, the ability to repeat actions proves high quality; hence, maturity is the highest level of skills in a given area of activity, considered from an attribute and functional perspective. It is naturally associated with incremental change, and is therefore a key concept in the theory of development, so universal that it refers not only to living organisms but to all phenomena that are characterized by the ability to develop (Skrzypek, 2022). The consequence of the above is the multidimensionality of maturity, which can be perceived in the biological context (maturity of living organisms), social (social maturity), as well as economic (maturity of the economy), market (maturity of markets and products), and technical (maturity of technology) (Skrzypek, 2013). From the point of view of management and quality sciences embedded in social sciences, all these dimensions are important, and what is more, a common denominator can be found for them – organization (Werner-Lewandowska and Kosacka-Olejnik, 2020).

Definitions of organizational maturity refer not only to the expected state but also often indicate the method of achieving subsequent levels or degrees of maturity.

It can therefore be concluded that the maturity of the management system is determined by the implementation of a specific management approach, management standard, process improvement methodology, self-assessment, information technology, and the adaptation of these elements to the adopted business model, which should take into account the specificity of the business and the adopted strategy (Skrzypek, 2022). According to Skrzypek's approach, maturity requires the professionalization of key organizational solutions and compliance with the best practices in organizational management.

Business maturity could be understood as a constant process of transformation, in which the knowledge that resides in the workers is the main piece needed to reach an optimum level of excellence (Moreno-Monsalve and Delgado-Ortiz, 2020). Basing maturity on human resources is one of the approaches; however, other researchers stress various aspects. For example, Raissi and Hakeem (2023) in their work refer to ISO practices. This approach is justified as the International Standards Organization has defined a standard approach to maturity and defined its levels. Hence, a standard-based approach may be a path towards organizational maturity. Implementing and maintaining standards is usually a consequence of having and cherishing a set of values, core values that constitute organizational culture. The cultural perspective on how personal and organizational maturity should be integrated into business activities is presented in the research by Herget (2023).

A culture-based approach is also explored in the research by Farzin Abdehgah et al. (2023). They analyze the literature on organizational maturity in the storytelling/narrative context. The results of their research identify areas to which organizational maturity is linked, namely healthcare (both in the context of biological/psychological maturity and the maturity of healthcare procedures and organizations), collective centering and collective sensemaking to express organizational culture, and identity and knowledge. These areas and topics are referred to in maturity definitions; hence, their occurrence in literature analysis on organizational maturity is justified. Literature analysis has also revealed a set of keywords corresponding to organizational maturity and maturity levels. These include identification (identification and assessment of maturity levels), systems (maturity of organization as a socio-technical system, and assessment system supporting maturity assessment), evolution (but also development and improvement – reaching maturity is, as mentioned before, an incremental process), performance (in the context of efficiency and improved performance), power (as a benefit from maturity, in the context of competitive advantage), and self (the most difficult to analyze, yet, showing that maturity assessment is self-centered). The results of the research by Farzin Abdehgah et al. (2023) focus on the qualitative approach to maturity and its assessment; however, they recognize the potential of qualitative research, both focused on understanding the concept (via qualitative and quantitative literature analysis) and its development (via contributing to new knowledge development, new models, and the generation of the assessment modes). Research on maturity and understanding maturity is more important because the more dynamic and challenging environments companies need to deal with, hence the need for academic and utilitarian research on the topic and the implementation of various perspectives on maturity development – both process and resource-oriented (Smite and Moe, 2023).

However, the multiplicity of definitions does not mean that the concept of maturity is ambiguous and blurry. When attempting to synthesize the concept of maturity, the following characteristics should be mentioned:

■ ability to achieve organizational goals,
■ ability to meet stakeholder expectations,
■ ability to improve.

These characteristics are the basis for developing maturity models.

1.2.2 Measuring and Assessing Maturity

The maturity model is a kind of maturity measurement scheme, where we define maturity as the organization's ability to continuously improve in a selected area. Assessment of the maturity of an organization is therefore a verification of the degree of achievement of perfection in the examined area, e.g., process management, quality management, and digitalization. The maturity assessment methodology takes quantitative and qualitative forms based on descriptions of practices and goals (Fraser and Gregory, 2002).

To determine the maturity level of an organization, the advancement of the management methods and techniques used throughout the organization is assessed.

Despite the popularity of the concept of maturity models, as pointed out by Wendler (2012), there is no clear definition of the term "maturity model" (Correia et al., 2017). A maturity model can be understood as "a conceptual framework consisting of parts that describe the development of a specific area of interest over time" (Pigosso et al., 2013). This definition assumes a comprehensive view of maturity models and does not limit it to a specific area (e.g., project or process management) (Correia et al., 2023).

The maturity model describes the current state and "offers a structured way of analyzing how an organization is meeting specific requirements and which areas require attention to achieve maturity levels" (Klimko, 2001). A maturity model is a conceptual framework consisting of parts that describe the development of a specific area of interest over time (Klimko, 2001) or state (Cuenca et al., 2013).

Maturity models aim to present gradual improvement in various areas, e.g., organization: organizational maturity models, process: process maturity model (Stachowiak and Pawłyszyn, 2021). The first maturity model relating to the area of management was Philip B. Crosby's model from 1979 (Crosby, 1979), and since that time numerous maturity models have been developed and implemented in many areas of organizational activity. In their research Sarmento dos Santos-Neto and Cabral Seixas Costa (2019) identified areas of maturity model implementation, i.e.:

- Software,
- Information management systems,
- Process management,
- Project management,
- Knowledge management,
- Sustainable development,
- Energy management,

- Risk management,
- Supply chains,
- Logistics,
- Education,
- Public sector,
- Construction and engineering,
- Services,
- Healthcare sector,
- Product lifecycle management,
- Research and development,
- Ergonomics

and many others, including:

- A model to evaluate the maturity of the integration of three management systems in the food industries, under the aspects of environment, quality, and food safety (Santos et al., 2022).
- Knowledge Management (KM) can improve the quality of products and services through the appropriate creation and sharing of organizational knowledge.
- KM models in organizational maturity processes, specifically with respect to the cycle of adoption of good project management practices (Moreno-Monsalve and Delgado-Ortiz, 2020).
- KM maturity assessment (Pires et al., 2021).
- Quality improvement maturity model is derived from holistic principles underlying the successful implementation of system-wide QI programs (Akmal et al., 2021).
- Maturity model for information and KM in the public sector is intended for use in frequent monitoring, trend analysis, and in-depth analysis of the contemporary information and KM practices of an organization (Jääskeläinen et al., 2022).
- IPMA Delta for assessing and developing project management maturity and the IPMA Organizational Competence Baseline, acting as a reference model for IPMA Delta (Bushuyev and Verenych, 2018).
- Assessment model for organizational business process maturity with a focus on BPM governance practices (de Boer et al., 2015).

Santos and Costa (2019) analyzed the models in the context of their validation and implementation. The structure of the models differs not necessarily in terms of the area they were designed for but mainly in terms of their purpose and implementation mode. Hence, there are maturity models that are used (De Bruin et al., 2005):

■ descriptive tool (to assess as is state),
■ prescriptive tool (to develop a road map for future improvement),
■ benchmarking tool (to compare with best practices and standards).

Maturity models also differ on account of their architecture. The first approach to the definition of the maturity model is called the top-to-bottom approach, and is based on a fixed number of maturity levels that are defined and characterized (Stachowiak and Pawłyszyn, 2021). The organization is assessed by comparing its individual characteristics with those presented in the model. An example of this approach are the maturity models by Becker et al. (2009), Gajsek et al. (2019), and Stachowiak and Oleśków-Szłapka (2018). Another approach, known as the bottom-to-top approach, is based on assessing previously determined characteristics and grouping the results. This approach, presented, e.g., by Lahrmann et al. (2011), is more flexible and adapted to the individual characteristics of the organization. Considering the number of maturity levels, it ranges from three to six, with five being the most common number of maturity levels (e.g., Pigosso et al., 2013; Golinska and Kuebler, 2014; Machado et al., 2017). According to Srai et al. (2013), this figure provides a sufficient level of detail to enable distinction between network maturity hierarchies, while still being accessible to the practitioner to make informed choices during the applied performance appraisal phases.

Some maturity models (e.g., Srai et al., 2013) do not include maturity level descriptors. Others, yes, but the descriptors are different for each maturity model. One of the common approaches is the universal concept presented by Edgeman and Eskildsen (2014), which includes very low maturity, low maturity, moderate maturity, high maturity, and very high maturity. Determining the maturity level requires assessing selected components. De Bruin et al. (2005) suggest that an extensive literature review can be used to identify both the components of the area being assessed and the subcomponents (detailed features). In order to identify mutually exclusive and jointly exhaustive areas, Mani et al. (2015) proposed three levels of analysis:

■ company's operation;
■ the inter-organizational level, where there are strong economic connections involving suppliers, customers, and consumers;
■ external level, which includes other external stakeholders such as the community, non-governmental organizations, and regulators.

The next step in building a maturity model is to explain how each area can be assessed (Correia et al., 2023) and how maturity can be measured. For this purpose, evaluation scales should be developed. There are various approaches that can be used, including:

- binary nominal scales – for decisions and answers "yes" or "no" and to facilitate the quantitative assessment process (grades 0 or 1) (e.g., Werner-Lewandowska, 2020);
- continuous, quantitative (e.g., increasing range 0–5, e.g., Golinska-Dawson et al., 2023) or qualitative (e.g., low, medium, high) scales (e.g., Looy et al., 2014).
- fuzzy numbers that reflect qualitative assessment in a more natural way, closer to natural language (Stachowiak and Pawłyszyn, 2021).

To visualize the various options and constructs of maturity assessment presented in the literature, selected models can be discussed in detail.

1.2.2.2 Capability Maturity Model Integration

CMMI (Capability Maturity Model Integration) was developed as part of the CMMI project, which aimed to increase the usability of maturity models by integrating many different models into one platform. CMMI is the successor to CMM (Capability Maturity Model) and related software. CMM was developed from 1987 to 1997, and in 2002 the first version of the model was published, developed by representatives of industry, government and the Carnegie Mellon Software Engineering Institute (SEI). The main sponsors of the project were: the Office of the Secretary of Defense (OSD) and the National Defense Industry Association. According to the Software Engineering Institute (SEI, 2009), CMMI helps "integrate traditionally separate organizational functions, establish goals and priorities for process improvement, provide guidance for quality processes, and provide a benchmark for evaluating current processes". In March 2016, the CMMI Institute was taken over by ISACA, the Information Systems Audit and Control Association. The CMMI model refers to process maturity – the maturity of processes is assessed. The model includes five levels of maturity: initial, managed, defined, quantitatively managed, and optimized.

1.2.2.3 Organizational Project Management Maturity Model

OPM3 (Organizational Project Management Maturity Model) was developed by PMI in late 2003. OPM (Organizational Project Management) is defined as the rational and logical use of knowledge, skills, tools, and techniques in organizational activities and design in order to achieve organizational goals through projects. The OPM3 model consists of four elements, including (Sorychta-Wojsczyk, 2018):

- Best Practices,
- Capabilities,
- Key Performance Indicators,
- Outcomes.

Best practices and skills – the main components of OPM3- fall into categories that make up the three dimensions of the model. Firstly, the model specifies domains – project, program, and portfolio management; secondly, after projects, programs, and portfolio, there is the OPM3 continuum – a process improvement process including the phases: standardization, measurement, control, and continuous improvement (SMCI) (Juchniewicz, 2016).

A characteristic feature of OPM3 is the modular structure of the standard, which allows for any scaling, selection of the necessary solutions, and adaptation to the needs of a given organization or just a small part of it. Like other PMI standards, OPM3 does not define an improvement path; however, it provides guidelines for achieving project management excellence by the organization. The model supports the achievement of maturity through a synergistic combination of knowledge, in the form of good practices, diagnosis, which will help to understand the current situation of the organization, identifying areas requiring attention, and improvement, which will help determine the steps needed to achieve performance improvement goals. Thus, it fits into both the diagnostic and prescriptive goals of maturity models.

1.2.2.4 IPMA Delta

The IPMA Delta model used to assess organizations is composed of modules based on leading project management standards:

- IPMA Competency Guidelines (ICB),
- Project Excellence Model (IPMA Project Excellence Model),
- ISO 21500.

IPMA Delta assesses the current state of the organization's competences in the field of project management (IPMA Delta competence class 1–5) and compares this assessment with the organization's own estimate of the competence class (through self-assessment). The effect is to define existing deviations (Delta). Identifying these areas of divergence helps pave the organization's path to a higher level of project management competency.

The assessment is carried out in three areas/modules (IPMA, 2019):

Module I – Individual competencies are assessed in key roles and perspectives: project, program and portfolio managers, project staff, senior management, administration and support functions. The assessment covers experience and knowledge in a given field and is carried out through self-assessment.

Module P (Projects) covers the evaluation of selected projects. The assessment focuses on the results and success of implemented projects and the use of appropriate project management methods and tools in the assessed projects. This module is also assessed through self-assessment.

Module O (Organization) includes the assessment of organizational competences in project management, from the point of view of top management, their attitude and support of the management system, as well as the establishment of management principles enabling efficient and effective implementation of projects.

The use of the model enables improvement in design and management competencies.

1.2.2.4.1 Portfolio, Program, and Project Management Maturity Model

P3M3 (Portfolio, Program, and Project Management Maturity Model) is a management maturity model that allows a holistic look at the organization in terms of how it implements its projects, programs, and portfolios of projects.

P3M3 is owned by Axelos, a joint venture between the UK government and multinational company Capita, which took over ownership in January 2014. It was previously owned by OGC (Office of Government Commerce), a branch of the UK government. The first version of the model was released in 2005, the next in 2008 and the next in 2015. The versions differ in their level of complexity.

The uniqueness of the model is that it does not focus only on processes but on the entire system. Moreover, assessment using the P3M3 model can and should be adapted to the actual needs of the organization and can be carried out in many different ways.

The model consists of three separate models that allow you to independently assess the maturity of the management of projects, programs, and portfolios without losing an overview of the relationship between these areas (Axelos, 2023).

Each of these models allows us to view the organization from seven perspectives: Organizational governance, Implementation control (in projects, programs, or portfolios, respectively), Benefits management, Risk management, Stakeholder management (engagement), Financial management, and Resource management.

The model distinguishes five maturity levels: initial, repeatable, defined, managed, and optimized. P3M3 is a model enabling the implementation of descriptive and prescriptive goals; it allows for a comprehensive assessment, similarly to the previous ones, referring to projects, programs, and portfolios.

1.2.2.5 Project Management Maturity Model

PMMM (Project Management Maturity Model) was developed by Harold Kerzner based on CMM. The model is static, which means that it allows for the identification of the maturity level of the organization.

The model describes five dimensions of project maturity (Juchniewicz, 2016):

- Level 1: Common language – participants know the importance of projects, have significant knowledge in the field of project management, and use the same deadlines in project implementation.
- Level 2: Shared Processes – the organization understands that shared processes must be defined and modified to replicate the success of one project in the next project.
- Level 3: Uniform methodology – the organization takes into account the synergistic effect of combining all methods in the organization into one methodology – its center is project management. The synergistic effect facilitates process control.
- Level 4: Benchmarking – the organization recognizes that process improvement is necessary to maintain a competitive advantage. Benchmarking should be a continuous process. The organization can decide what to learn and from whom to learn it.
- Level 5: Continuous improvement – the organization continuously evaluates the information obtained from benchmarking and decides whether this information is useful for improving its project management method.

The project maturity assessment process, according to the PMM model, uses a questionnaire consisting of simple questions. The answers provided are compared with a developed key that indicates the level of maturity of the organization. The simplicity of the assessment is an advantage of Kerzner's model; it enables self-assessment and reduces the costs associated with the diagnosis of maturity (Juchniewicz, 2009).

The PMM model was used by James S. Pennypacker and Kevin P. Grant in their 2002 conference paper (Pennypacker and Grant, 2002), one of the most authoritative and most cited studies on the topic.

1.2.2.6 Project Management Maturity Model

ProMMM (Project Management Maturity Model) was developed by D. Hillson in 2001, to meet the needs of organizations by offering a maturity model that can act as a reference point for capabilities (Hillson, 2003; Hillson and Timerick, 2001). Its structure is based on elements of existing models, such as the Capability Maturity Model (CMM) and the EFQM Excellence Model. ProMMM is a practical and pragmatic model, based on empirical experience in project management. The lack of an academic research base is not seen as a disadvantage because ProMMM represents the accumulated knowledge of project management professionals who are leading practitioners in the field.

ProMMM has four levels, with specific steps along the way against which organizations can compare themselves. ProMMM has been used by many large organizations to benchmark their project management processes as part of an improvement initiative, across a variety of industry sectors including: construction, nuclear, public sector, telecommunications, defense, pharmaceuticals and engineering. It offers a general framework for assessing project management capabilities in organizations in any industry, including those responsible for FM projects, and is not dependent on prior achievement of a specific level of the project management process (Hillson, 2003).

The Project Management Maturity Model (ProMMM) is composed of four maturity levels, defined as naive, novice, standardized, and natural. The goal is to provide a structured path to project management excellence with defined steps that organizations can follow. The levels can be summarized as follows (Hillson, 2001):

■ Level 1: A naive project management organization is not aware of the need for project management and does not have a structured approach to projects. Management processes are iterative and reactive, with little or no attempt to learn from the past or prepare for future threats or uncertainties.

- Level 2: An emerging project management organization has begun to experiment with project management, perhaps through a small number of nominated people, but does not have any formal or structured overall processes. The Novice organization, although aware of the potential benefits of project management, has not effectively implemented project management processes and is not realizing the full benefits.
- Level 3: Standardized project management organization. At this level, project management is implemented in all aspects of the enterprise. Overall, project management processes are formalized and common, and the benefits are understood at all levels of the organization, although they may not be fully realized in all cases.
- Level 4: Natural organization of project management. In this case, the organization has a fully project-based culture, with a proactive approach to project management in all aspects of the business. Project-based information is actively used to improve business processes and gain a competitive advantage.

Each level of ProMMM is further defined in terms of four attributes, namely (Hillson, 2001): culture, process, experience, and usage.

They allow an organization to evaluate its current project management processes against established criteria, set realistic improvement goals, and measure progress towards increasing project management capabilities. Four attributes were selected to represent the areas required for effective project management, reflecting the common belief that tools and training are not sufficient enablers.

1.2.2.7 Software Process Improvement and Capability Determination

SPICE (Software Process Improvement and Capability Determination) is an international standard for the evaluation of software processes developed jointly by ISO (International Organization for Standardization) and IEC (International Electrotechnical Commission). SPICE is described in the ISO/IEC 15504 standard. It is a group of technical standards documents relating to the computer software development process and related business management functions.

The process is assessed in terms of the methods, tools, and practices that are used to develop and test software. The purpose of process evaluation is to detect areas for improvement and to propose improvement solutions.

The SPICE model is composed of six maturity levels (Goździewska-Nowiska and Janicki, 2021): incomplete, performed, managed, established, predictable, and optimized.

The model is used to analyze five basic types of processes: customer-supplier, engineering, design, support, and organization. Quantification of the maturity level takes place thanks to the so-called process attributes, such as (Goździewska-Nowicka and Janicki, 2021) process efficiency, process innovation, and process control.

Maturity measurement is usually based on the architecture of maturity models. When measuring maturity, other aspects can be assessed in parallel, e.g., RandD works and readiness of RandD organizations, since maturity is multidimensional and may reflect other organizational characteristics as well (Melnyk and Nikitin, 2021). It is also possible to evaluate the organizational maturity of asset owners from the perspectives of the activity systems and BIM (building information modeling) governance dimensions of people, process, and technology (Munir et al., 2020), combined with readiness for potential disruptive innovations based on past and current conditions ("disruptive susceptibility") (Klenner et al., 2013).

1.2.2.8 Sustainable Logistics Management Maturity

In their research, Werner-Lewandowska and Golinska-Dawson developed and tested the model related to sustainable development and sustainability, focusing on sustainable logistics management. The model's architecture includes five maturity levels for sustainable logistics management, and the model's scope is the assessment of logistics management in the context of sustainable developed dimensions (economic, environmental, and social). The assessment is based on literature derived, and experts proved a list of 36 assessment criteria that are logistics tools having an impact on three dimensions of sustainable development. The strength of the impact is reflected in the weight of the factors. Assessment is conducted based on the four-step procedure: (1) Data collection, (2) Calculation of a Sustainable Logistics Management Indicator for each dimension of sustainability, (3) Calculation of an Overall Sustainable Logistics Management Indicator, and (4) Identification of maturity level. Hence, the procedure enables the identification of the OSLMI (Overall Sustainable Logistics Management Indicator), which indicates the level of maturity, but it also enables the analysis of logistics maturity in the context of selected dimensions of sustainable development.

The assessment is based on observations in the company and questionnaires for logistics managers. Thanks to them, it is possible to identify logistics tools, and based on their list, it is possible to assess logistics management maturity in a sustainable development context. The data required is the impact of each tool on sustainable development dimensions. Defining maturity levels in the area of sustainable logistics management results from the assumption made in the research that the logistics tools used translate into the management decisions aimed at implementing a sustainable development strategy in each of its dimensions.

1.2.2.9 Digital Logistics Process Maturity (DITILOGPRO)

Digitalization is one of the key issues when striving for competitive advantage; hence, digital maturity assessment is one of the research topics interesting from an academic and practical perspective. In their research Golinska-Dawson et al. (2023) developed and implemented the Digital Logistics Process Maturity Model. Their model is structured into five levels of maturity, defined as follows:

■ ML1 (Avoidance) – the frequency of implementing high-intelligence digital solutions in logistics processes is very low.
■ ML2 (Discovery) – the frequency of implementing high-intelligence digital solutions in logistics processes is low.
■ ML3 (Adoption) – the frequency of adaptation of high-intelligence digital solutions for logistics processes is average.
■ ML4 (Improvement) – the frequency of implementing high-intelligence digital solutions in logistics processes is high.
■ ML5 (Excellent) – the frequency of implementing high-intelligence digital solutions in logistics processes is very high.

The scope of the assessment covers the frequency of using advanced digital solutions during the implementation of logistics processes, while the list of advanced digital solutions (evaluation criteria) includes high-intelligence digital solutions such as Blockchain DLT solution, Intelligent Transport Systems (ITS), Robotic Processes Automation (RPA), IoT, Big Data Analytics, Cloud, and APIs. Digital tools are rated in terms of the frequency of their use in logistics processes on a scale of 0–5 based on the responses of managers responsible for investment and development decision-making. The assessment procedure is based on three steps: (1) Data collection, (2) Maturity Index calculation, and (3) Maturity level identification.

The assessment is based on responses to questionnaires for managers. Thanks to them, it is possible to identify advanced digital tools, and based on their list, it is possible to assess logistic maturity in the digitization context.

1.2.2.10 Logistics 4.0/Industry 4.0 Maturity Model

Digitization is one of the aspects of Industry 4.0, the set of solutions dedicated to manufacturing companies. A similar approach is implemented for logistics processes and is referred to as Logistics 4.0. In their research, Batz et al. (2020) develop and implement the Logistics4.0 Maturity Model. The model is used to identify Logistics 4.0 solutions used in enterprises in relation to management, material flow, and information flow. The model includes five levels of maturity, namely:

- Ignoring: at this level, the company does not see the need to integrate flows and has no knowledge of advanced solutions that improve the flow of materials and information.
- Defining: at this level, the company recognizes the need for integration, but does not know how to achieve it; it has knowledge of advanced solutions that improve the flow of materials and information but does not use them.
- Adoption: at this level, the company initiates integration and implements selected advanced solutions that improve the flow of materials and information.
- Management: at this level, most areas are already integrated, and the company has implemented numerous advanced solutions to improve the flow of materials and information.
- Integration: at this level, the integration of all areas and flows gives a synergy effect, all possible advanced solutions to improve the flow of materials and information are implemented.

Maturity assessment is carried out in three aspects: it concerns the implementation of material and information flows (based on classic logistics definitions) and management.

In the L4MM model, the maturity assessment procedure is based on a questionnaire that includes questions relating to the implementation of material and information flows. The questions do not indicate specific solutions, but only their advanced nature according to the following guidelines:

In the area of management, maturity is demonstrated by planned and implemented investments, innovation management, and the integration of value chains.

In the area of material flow, maturity is demonstrated by the automation and robotization of processes in the warehouse and internal logistics, as well as the implementation of solutions such as IoT, 3D printing, and augmented reality.

In the area of information flow, maturity is demonstrated by advanced IT systems and the use of BigData and RTLS systems.

To identify implemented solutions and tools a simple questionnaire was designed with seven questions presented to managers at logistics companies:

1. Do you know the terms Logistics 4.0 and Industry 4.0?
2. Are you familiar with the term Internet of Things and/or Services?
3. Is your warehouse automated?
4. Are your internal logistics processes automated?
5. Is data flow and access to information integrated in real time?
6. Do you analyze, store and process data using modern technologies (i.e. Bigdata, cloud computing)?
7. Do you use RTLS in your logistics processes?

The answers to the questions were structured in a way that allowed them to be assigned to maturity levels.

■ I don't know, I have never heard of the respondent being placed at level 1 (ignoring).
■ I know, but I don't use it places the respondent at level 2 (defining).
■ I know and partially uses it places the respondent at level 3 (adaptation).
■ I know and use all possibilities in this area. Places the respondent at level 4 (management).

The maturity level of an organization is determined by the predominant number of responses at a given level.

Achieving level 5 (integrating) is only possible when all answers indicate the full use of the potential of Logistics 4.0 solutions.

Batz et al. (2020) used the model to evaluate a certain population of enterprises, however, it can also be used for individual evaluation. The use of the interview form may then be supplemented by observation or document review.

1.2.2.11 Online Maturity Assessment

One of the examples of online maturity assessment offered by the BPM Institute focused on digital maturity (https://www.bpminstitute.org/organizational-digital-maturity-assessment). The form available online focuses on six areas:

- Culture
- Customer experience
- Business process
- Digital technologies
- Agile
- Business Architecture

These areas are not all that could be considered, yet they are identified as crucial. The following skills are central to success in these six practice areas:

1. Viewing the business from the outside-in: The customer's point of view is an essential skill in improving the customer experience.
2. Being able to assess and improve enterprise processes: An indispensable skill in optimizing how value is created for the company and its customers.
3. Understanding how to integrate various digital technologies: Optimal impact is a vital skill to nurture.
4. Enabling an agile approach to deploying technology: A needed skill set in this day and age.
5. Representing the company's strategy in an architecture: That's implementable in IT terms is central to success.
6. A cohesive amalgamation of the above skill sets: Is it important to adopt a digital business culture?

Another tool for digital maturity assessment is the one offered by Gartner (https://www.gartner.com/en/conferences/emea/digital-workplace-uk/conference-resources/digital-maturity-assessment?utm_source=googleandutm_medium=cpcandutm_campaign=EVT_EMEA_2024_PCCE19_CPC_SEM1_DSAandutm_adgroup=159789090644andutm_term=andad=68889 9028720andmatchtype=andgad_source=1andgclid=CjwKCAiA0bWvBhBjEiwAt EsoW9HGfbvxlRUi_wNGtghDCj6USL4dnNsEEhXo6jVVOK1JmyeLTdVQnxoC-SpYQAvD_BwE). It is focused on workplace digital maturity and offers some guidelines for recognizing the level of maturity and supporting the transition to higher levels, e.g., attending conferences and workshops.

Another example of an online maturity assessment is the one provided by PWC (Price Waterhouse Coopers). The tool is available online, but it is not free since it is supported with some consulting (https://www.pwc.com/sk/en/digital-solutions/maturity-asessment.html). The methodology of assessment is a seven-step procedure:

1. Analysis of selected areas,
2. Mapped current processes with recommendations for increasing efficiency,
3. Maturity assessment of selected areas to compare yourself to other players in the industry,
4. Strategic recommendations,
5. Training plan for your staff based on identified gaps,
6. Implementation plan for tackling improvements in a systematic manner,
7. High-level business case.

And covers the following areas:

■ Workforce assessment,
■ Shopfloor assessment,
■ Value stream mapping,
■ Equipment efficiency.

It is also possible to include:

■ Stockkeeping and portfolio management,
■ Maintenance optimization,
■ Quality improvement.

Expected benefits from assessment and further guidance/consulting include: cost reduction – a maturity assessment can help you identify opportunities for cost reduction in multiple areas; overall maturity assessment – health check of your business in core areas; revenue growth – identifying gaps, bottlenecks, and opportunities for improvement; high level business case and implementation plan – how to tackle improvements in a systematic manner.

1.2.3 Conclusion

Generally, companies are striving for a high level of maturity; however, a high level of organizational maturity and hierarchy can be a blocker to adaptability to change if the organization stays on the single-loop of learning (does perfectly what it used to do). Mistakes are accepted and thanks to this, learning from mistakes also supports organizational change adaptability. Change adaptability is vital for double-loop learning (organizational action re-framing) (Kucharska, 2021). Some works also refer to triple-loop learning for projects that forms the basis of a new framework, adding development/dynamic perspective to the basic approach (McClory et al., 2017).

Various levels of maturity can be used as a background for other research topics, e.g., skills required (Benbasat et al., 1980) or processes performed, i.e., servitization process (Baines et al., 2020), compliance and safety/security issues (Kwon and Johnson, 2013), or the use of advanced scheduling systems, which prove to be valuable for mature organizations only (Ivert and Jonsson, 2014), or management control systems (Haustein et al., 2014). Moreover, leadership competencies are positively associated with key operational performance indicators, organizational maturity level of lean, and leaders' experience with lean systems (Seidel et al., 2017), and organizational maturity seems to be crucial for technology implementation and adoption (Yoon and Lim, 2010).

1.3 Resilience

1.3.1 Resilience Is the Key!

The term resilience gained specific attention and importance during and after the pandemic. Resilience was the feature expected from individuals, societies, and organizations. Their well-being and, in many cases, survival depended on their characteristics; hence, identification of these characteristics became a focal point of research in many areas, starting with medicine but also reaching into management and business studies. A resilient organization is the one that demonstrates "long-term development capacity and good economic condition despite changes in external conditions" (Romanowska, 2012). The aspect of long-term, stable (and therefore sustainable) development is consistent with the considerations regarding contemporary requirements for management and organization presented in the previous chapter, as is the variability of the environment included in the definition.

Resilience is "a certain property of an organization enabling its survival and sustainable development, which is built, on the one hand, by the organization's insusceptibility and insensitivity to the impact of crisis-generating factors, enabling the avoidance of problems and difficulties, and, on the other hand, by the ability to resist the impact of these factors (i.e. the ability of the organization to respond to their occurrence, regardless of their location (external, internal), i.e., in fact, the ability of the organization to maintain its integrity (survive) and operate correctly (satisfactory) during the impact of crisis factors, or the state of the organization conditioned by the entirety of management processes aimed at restoring the integrity of its internal environment (i.e., in fact, ensuring durability and sustainable development), disturbed by factors of a crisis-generating nature" (Zabłocka-Kluczka, 2012).

The term itself was recognized before the pandemic, and the first research was identified in the Scopus database in 1992, yet the academic interest in the topic was limited. Only in 2019 did it start to grow dynamically, proving that research on resilience is important and that incremental increase in knowledge in the field is valuable from not only an academic but also a utilitarian perspective. The introduction of the terms and literature on resilience presented in the chapter is based on an analysis of 696 papers on organizational resilience indexed in the Scopus database in the field of business and management. The most cited and latest publications were analyzed in the greatest detail to reflect the most recognized and contemporary approaches used in organizational resilience studies (Figure 1.3).

An analysis of the literature in the field is presented in the figure developed based on an analysis of abstracts and keywords of publications on resilience in the field of business and management. Implementation of VosViewer led to the identification of nine clusters, stressing the importance of capability (brown cluster), as undoubtedly resilience is a capability of an organization, and resilience mechanism (orange cluster), as resilience is about surviving in difficult conditions/environments, and the mechanism of survival is interesting as it can be imitated by others. An interesting area is the one referred to as social capital and family firms (turquoise cluster), as due to strong internal links and a specific approach to business they tend to be more resilient than others. Performance (purple cluster) is an area of specific interest as lower performance is quite often a consequence of disturbances and distractions emerging from both internal and external crises;

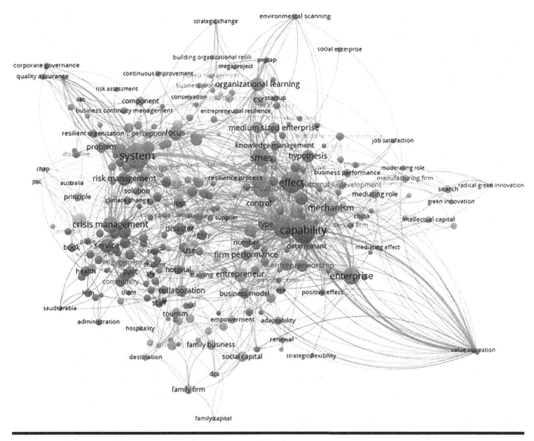

Figure 1.3   Resilience in literature: semantic map based on publications identified in the Scopus database (retrieved: December 1, 2023).

Source: Developed with VosViewer.

hence, interest in effects (blue cluster) is also high. Counteracting the difficulties and surviving requires a systemic approach and integration (green cluster) and transparency of functioning (yellow cluster), strengthened with the support of crisis management (red cluster).

The most often cited, and hence the most recognized research on organizational resilience focuses on the sources of resilience. Lengnick-Hall et al. (2011), in their research, suggest that resilience is the result of strategically managing human resources to create competencies among core employees. They identified three elements central to developing an organization's capacity for resilience (specific cognitive abilities, behavioral characteristics, and contextual conditions) and related them to the individual attitudes and behaviors of employees. Their key finding was that HR policies can influence employees and their individual contributions, which, when aggregated through the processes of double interaction and attraction-selection-attrition, may lead to possess a capacity for resilience. The link and interrelation between individual and organizational resilience was also identified in the research by Bhamra et al. (2011), in which they analyzed available literature on the topic, identifying the term, its application, and a number of areas for advancing resilience research, in particular: the relationship between human and organizational resilience; understanding interfaces between organizational and infrastructural resilience. As human resources are an important component of sustainability (they are a social pillar, which is a construct complementing economic and environmental ones), the sustainability aspect is also considered when analyzing organizational resilience. In their work Ortiz-de-Mandojana and Bansal (2016) suggest that social and environmental practices contribute to organizational resilience defined as a company's ability to sense and correct maladaptive tendencies and cope positively with unexpected situations. Their research is valuable as it covers a 15-year period, which provides a long-term perspective crucial in recognizing both the sustainability of operations and organizational resilience. They found that companies that adopt responsible social and environmental practices have lower financial volatility, higher sales growth, and higher chances of survival. A similar approach was taken by DesJardine et al. (2019). They also focused on the role of social and environmental business practices in contributing to *organizational resilience*, even though they recognized difficulties in measuring organizational resilience. To cope with the problem, they introduced two ways in which organizational resilience manifests. The first of them, severity of loss, captures the stability dimension of resilience, while the second, time to recovery, captures the flexibility dimension. The conclusion offered is that strategic social and environmental practices contribute more to *organizational resilience* than tactical social and environmental practices. Another aspect considered is presented by Duchek et al. (2020) and focused on developing resilience, yet, sustainability is not considered. The approach taken is based on a process approach and deconstructing resilience into three stages, including anticipation, coping, and adaptation. The author identifies capabilities that form organizational resilience, discussing its antecedents and drivers. The research by Burnard and Bhamra (2011) also strives to define a conceptual framework for organizational resilience trying to characterize the response of an organization to disruptive events. Again, a process-oriented approach is implemented as the authors aim to outline the fundamental processes that make organizations resilient and enable resilient responses to disruptive events. A process-oriented approach manifests itself also via change-embracing. The research by Ates and Bititci (2011) suggests continuous change and improvement as key drivers of innovative responses to the market that prove the sustainability and/or resilience of organizations. Ates and Bititci suggest that instilling, developing, and implementing change capabilities is paramount to making progress towards sustainability and resilience, especially for SMEs. Their research results prove that sustainability and resilience in SMEs are enhanced by (1) the ability to embrace organizational and people dimensions, as well as operational aspects of change management, and (2) paying attention to long-term planning and external communication to drive change proactively. Exploring the antecedents and drivers of organizational resilience seems to be interesting from both academic and utilitarian perspectives, hence the case-based research by Pal et al. (2014). They identified the antecedents of resilience, and their different degrees of impact on organizations. In their research, Pal et al. focused on small and medium enterprises that are especially threatened by economic disturbances/crises. Through the research conducted, they deepened their understanding of the underlying patterns in the antecedents, favoring or inhibiting resilience due to their significance or deficit. The key enablers of resilience identified in their research include resourcefulness, relational networks, and material assets, as well as "dynamic competitiveness" through strategic and operational flexibility, together with the indirect influence of attentive leadership and collectiveness. The most important aspect of resilience was the economic one; hence, financial performance, mostly through the generation of profitability, cash flow/liquidity, and sales turnover were considered the effects expected. The patterns recognized to utilize and direct the antecedents for resilience were simply growth and continuity strategies. Since resilience is generally perceived from a long-term perspective, a strategic approach is usually implemented. Annarelli and Nonino (2016), however, conducted research on the strategic and operational management of organizational resilience. Their research was theoretical; they aimed to find the solutions already existing in the literature, yet what they found was a research gap. The systematic literature review conducted confirmed that there is a commonly accepted definition of resilience, its foundations, and characteristics, whereas the literature is still far from offering solutions for the implementation of resilience, the patterns for how to reach operational resilience, and how to create and maintain resilient processes. The work was published in 2016 and is one of the most cited, being the inspiration for further research on organizational resilience. Resilience is an organizational characteristic needed and required in many situations. Its importance in economic crises was proved by Pal et al. (2014), while research on the importance of organizational resilience in responding to the impacts of extreme weather events was conducted by Linnenluecke and Griffiths (2012). They based their research on the assumption that more frequent and severe weather extremes such as heat waves, hurricanes, flooding, and droughts will have an increasing impact on organizations, industries, and entire economies. As a result, they developed a comprehensive conceptual framework for organizational adaptation and resilience to extreme weather events based on the anticipatory mechanisms and adaptation patterns. Win et al. (2011) also stressed the consequences of climate change on organizations: the more severe, the less organizations are aware of the organizational impacts of more and increasingly intense storms, floods, droughts, fires, and sea level rise. In their research, Win et al. identify dimensions of climate impacts such as severity, temporal scale, spatial scale, predictability, mode, immediacy, state change potential, and accelerating trend potential that altogether contribute to hyperturbulence in organizational environments. To deal with the conditions listed above, management of sustainability, crisis, risk, resilience, and adaptive organizational is required and consequently addressed in the paper.

Another disturbance recognized as a key motivator for organizational resilience was the COVID-19 pandemic. Filimanou and Coteau (2020) examined the impact of the pandemic on organizations, specifically *organizational resilience* and the extent of CSR practices. According to Filimanou et al., organizational response to COVID-19 affects perceived job security and enhances managers' organizational commitment, presenting resilience as an important concept explaining how organizations can survive and thrive in turbulent conditions. The conclusion from their research is consistent with other research on the topic – operational issues, and specifically resilience assessment and measurement, should be more explored. Trying to fill in the research gap, they suggested an approach to resilience measurement. Another approach to resilience measurement was presented by Somers (2009) in a relatively early stage of research on resilience. The concept is based on pro-active, rather than reactive, dealing with crises via a crisis plan. The new paradigm suggested is based on creating organizational structures and processes that build *organizational resilience* potential. The result of the research is a scale to measure latent resilience in organizations. Considering resilience as a pro-active approach naturally links the term with entrepreneurship. The systematic literature review on the co-existence of these two management concepts is presented in the paper by Korber and McNaughton (2018). The following relationships were identified: (1) resilience as a trait or characteristic of entrepreneurial firms or individuals, (2) resilience as a trigger for entrepreneurial intentions, (3) entrepreneurial behavior as enhancing *organizational resilience*, (4) entrepreneurial firms fostering macro-level (regions, communities, economies) resilience, (5) resilience in the context of entrepreneurial failure, and (6) resilience as a process of recovery and transformation. Links and intersections were found yet considered unsatisfactory from a research perspective, hence recognizing the potential of employing entrepreneurship in resilience development from both a theoretical and utilitarian point of view was suggested. One of the first publications addressing the implementation of organizational resilience is the one by Mallak (1998), according to which an organization that is resilient needs people who can respond quickly and effectively to change while enduring minimal stress. Human factors and adaptation capabilities are the basis of the concept, and this approach has been confirmed in research conducted in the last 25 years; however, the number of factors that make organizations resilient is increasing nowadays. Sullivan-Taylor and Branicki (2011) in their research indicate the importance of adaptation and flexibility, yet the results of research conducted among large and small and medium companies lead to the conclusion that organizational solutions leading to resilience may differ on account of the size of a company. The perspective of SMEs was also taken by Herbane (2019) in original research that led to the identification of four clusters: Attentive Interventionists, Light Planners, Rooted Strategists, and Reliant Neighbors, shaped by historical, developmental, and strategic factors. The publication presents associations between resilience and social capital, examines how locational choices generate a proximity premium, and develops a growth-survival-maturity perspective on SME resilience, revealing links between entrepreneurial activities and decisions about planning, networks, learning, and location. Moreover, employing different perspectives may lead to new conclusions as well, King et al. (2016) in their research took the perspective of workplace resilience and its impact on organizations. Another new concept is presented by Kantur and İşeri-Say (2012), who identify organizational evolvability, which is the outcome of organizational resilience, emphasizing the heightened sensitivity and increased wisdom of the post-event organization. They develop a model in which sources of *organizational resilience* are categorized as perceptual stance, contextual integrity, strategic capacity and strategic acting. The latest research on resilience needs to consider many factors not recognized before, including the post-Covid economy, wars and psychosocial crises combined with high inflation rates and the degression of the economy. Ghanem and Ghaley (2024) explore the resilience of public-private partnerships together with the Social Capital Theory and the organization resilience models described in the literature. Searching for support and building alliances is a well-established approach recognized from both theoretical and utilitarian perspective, indirectly connected with the triple (multiple?) helix concept. On the other hand, Kou et al. (2024) focus on factors influencing organizational resilience employing machine learning algorithms. In their research they identify the key characteristics of a resilient company and their specific impact patterns. The conclusion they reach is that stability during the crisis depends more on the pre-crisis company's operating conditions, while the post-crisis flexibility depends more on the internal and external resources. Research results provide empirical evidence on how managers can better respond to systemic crises and enhance organizational resilience. Even though discussion on organizational resilience has been presented in scientific literature many times, there is still a need to explore the topic. In the research by Tekletsion et al. (2024), organizational resilience is perceived as a paradoxical management, which is evidenced by the analysis of the papers in which opposite but interrelated demands or paradox elements are recognized in the conceptualization of resilience. The research does not undermine the definition of resilience as the ability of organizations to anticipate, survive, and thrive through shocks or the capability of anticipating, coping with, and recovering from unexpected events and adversities, yet it critically examines the literature for indications of paradoxical tensions within discussing the processes of resilience. Prayag et al. (2024) take a more traditional perspective using the disaster/crisis management cycle (DMC) to explore how dynamic capabilities (DCs) build and sustain organizational resilience. Their research reveals that threats and opportunities presented by the COVID-19 pandemic activated 10 different types of DCs (replicating, integrating, reconfiguring, creating, developing, assimilating, renewing, adaptive, innovative, and regenerative) across all the stages of resilience, response (short-term) and future recovery intentions (long-term) stages of resilience. Another study by Prayag et al. (2024), employing conservation of resources (COR) theory, identified the effect of leadership behaviors on resilience. The resilient leadership behaviors include vision sharing, leadership of tasks, and management of change, and supplement them with employee resilience (cognitive, behavioral, and contextual) and *organizational resilience* (planned and adaptive). The research results in the conclusion that contextual and behavioral dimensions of employee resilience mediate the effect of resilient leadership behaviors on organizational resilience. Safari et al. (2024), on the other hand, focused on structural aspects and conducted a systematic literature review and analysis of resilience in the context of supply chains, SMEs, and start-ups. They identified collaboration and networking and risk management as the most crucial resilience capabilities for all firms, whereas lean and quality management principles and utilizing information technology were crucial for SMEs and KM and contingency planning for large companies. Various approaches and patterns are recognized, and various situations are perceived as positive or negative. For example, in Kim and Hyun (2024) research, pandemics were recognized as phenomena having both negative and positive effects, and organizational resilience was the way to turn negative impacts into positive *results*. The novelty of the research lies in the synthesis of three distinct perspectives: attribute, process, and multi-level, which were merged into a unified model, identifying precursors of resilience at different levels. The approach presented by Bartel and Rockmann (2024) discusses various perspectives as it employs an attention-based view to theorize how different patterns of attention are associated with configurations of structures for building interpersonal relationships. They argue that relational indifference may result in weakening *organizational resilience*. Human resources and capabilities were the perspectives often taken when recognizing and developing resilience, yet relations and attention issues were not discussed, and that research gap was filled in by Bartel and Rockmann. Another original perspective is the one presented by Gómez et al. (2024), even though the starting point for their research is a traditional one. In their research, RBV and ergodicity are the basis, together with an assumption that organizational resilience depends on certain key characteristics of companies and their ability to innovate their business models. However, they focus on female leadership and a multi-unit structure. They find these two characteristics to be the ones that may condition the resilience emerging from resource availability and the ability to perform innovative actions. Considering substantial changes in the market and new knowledge generated in the management field, Khan et al. (2024) aim to redefine the concept of organizational resilience and present a new updated framing of resilience definition using categorization of attributes under process, structure and strategic move/action, emanating from a cross-disciplinary foundation. They exploit social, mechanical, and ecological literature regarding the construct of resilience to present it in the most comprehensive way possible, and finally, they present a new frame-based methodological approach for presenting the attributes and subordinate concepts of resilience. Ciasullo et al. (2024) also review literature, but they focus on linking resilience and sustainability. The approach was implemented before, yet there is a substantial growth in requirements for sustainability and the implementation of sustainable development goals. Hence, Ciasullo et al. present an eco-social interpretation of organizational resilience, and confront it with environmental sustainability. Their research leads to the conclusion that management actions to build organizational resilience should follow an ecosystem sustainability orientation that is based on embedding the firm in an eco-social setting and emphasizing its homeostatic exchanges with the environment. A similar concept is presented by Ma and Liu (2024), as they explore corporate social responsibility (CSR) principles in the context of resilience building. The subject of their research is project-based organizations, specific to the organizational conditions they operate in. They identify six paths to building high and low resilience in project-based organizations (PBOs) and the driving mechanisms of high and low resilience. Hence, their study verifies the relationship between CSR fulfillment and PBO resilience, revealing its mechanisms and paths; moreover, it provides a new approach to organizational resilience. Another perspective is offered by Douglas and Haley (2024), since their research is to analyze the conceptual and domain overlap of organizational learning and organizational resilience, as learning is basically the way to adapt to changes, both on an individual and organizational level. The results of the research are the strategies to foster collective learning leading to organizational resilience that were identified and outlined. Learning is based on pre-established patterns that allow reactions in a planned and organized way, and since resilience is about dealing with the unpredictable, sometimes it may not be enough. Thus, the research by Shela et al. (2024) introduces the concept of improvisation. Improvisation capability is not sufficiently discussed in the literature, hence the need to discuss the latest strategies to foster improvisation capability to amplify organizational resilience. Shela et al. identify the pertinent role of improvisation capability in amplifying organizational resilience and discuss various feasible strategies to cultivate organizational improvisation capability offering a new and original approach to organizational resilience. Combining learning and improvisation creates a space for discussing intellectual capital as a driving force in building organizational resilience. The research by Li and Lin (2024) proves that flexible human resources management systems are positively correlated with intellectual capital and organizational resilience. According to Li and Lin, Intellectual capital mediates the link between flexible human resources management systems and organizational resilience. Implementation of the RBV and the theory of dynamic capabilities is a new contribution to the organizational resilience field, and digital capability is introduced as a situational factor for understanding the effect of intellectual capital on organizational resilience. Recent works on organizational resilience are strongly affected by the pandemic, but they also benefit from the increased knowledge in the field.

1.3.2 Measuring and Assessing Resilience

To measure resilience, it is crucial to understand its nature. The literature does not give an exact answer and offers various definitions of resilience, as evidenced in the previous chapter; however, for the measurement purposes, two general approaches can be distinguished, namely:

■ Static approach, in which resilience is perceived as a result of specific actions (Sincorá et al., 2008; Weick, 1996; Gittell et al., 2006) or a function of an organization (Wicker & Breuer, 2013; McManus et al., 2008);
■ Dynamic approach, in which resilience is a capability (i.e., Duchek et al., 2020; Koronis and Ponis, 2018; Kim et al., 2016) or a process (i.e., Ishak and Williams, 2018; Lengnick-Hall et al., 2011; Allen and Toder, 2004).

The approach accepted determines the procedure for resilience measurement. There are various measures of resilience, including (Chen et al., 2021):

■ two factors measures (focused on (1) planning ability and (2) adaptability or (1) organizational awareness and (2) adaptability);
■ three factors measures (focused on (1) organizational resources, (2) organizational learning and (3) organizational adaptation, or (1) organizational learning ability, (2) adaptability and (3) dynamic ability, or (1) structural dependence, (2) organizational capacity and (3) process continuity, or (1) robustness, (2) agility, and (3) integrity, or (1) situational awareness, (2) critical vulnerability management, and (3) adaptability);
■ four factors measures (focused on (1) robustness, (2) redundancy, (3) adequacy, and (4) speediness, or (1) structural ability, (2) cognitive ability, (3) relational ability, and (4) emotional ability, or (1) expected competencies, (2) adaptive culture, (3) network competency, and (4) organizational learning).

Measuring and assessing resilience requires considering various aspects, including structural and dynamic ones.

1.3.2.1 Organizational Resilience in British Standard

Organizational resilience is defined by the BS 65000 standard as "the ability of an organization to anticipate, prepare for, respond to, and adapt to incremental change and sudden disruptions in order to survive and prosper". The standard provides a model and assessment mode that can be used by multiple organizations.

The model, referred to as a BSI Organizational Resilience framework, presents a dynamic approach based on four phases:

1. survive: survive the crises.
2. stabilize: stabilize operations in new conditions.
3. rebuilt: rebuilt in new conditions.
4. resilient: operate in new conditions.

The assessment mode based on the BSI Organizational Resilience Framework covers four categories, namely: leadership, people, process, and product, split into 16 elements, including: leadership, vision and purpose, reputational risk, financial management, resource management, culture, community engagement, awareness and training, alignment, governance and accountability, business continuity, supplier management, information and KM, horizon scanning, innovation, and adaptive capacity.

The perceived performance is measured across all the elements on a scale of 1–10, starting from the lowest. The results of the assessment can be benchmarked by sector, size, and longevity.

The approach introduced in BS was modified and implemented by the researchers from the University of Cranfield. They conducted their research on organizational resilience in 2017 and 2018 using 16 predefined elements of organizational resilience, divided into four groups:

■ Leadership: leadership, vision and purpose, reputational risk, financial management, resource management.
■ People: culture, community engagement, awareness, training and testing, alignment.
■ Processes: knowledge and information, supply chain, business continuity, management, and responsibility.
■ Product: adaptability, innovation, horizon monitoring.

The above categories have been defined based on international standards and best practices: British Standards Organizational Resilience Guidance (BS 65000:2014, 2014), Organizational Governance Guidance (BS 13500), Information Security Standards (ISO/IEC 27001), Security and durability – organizational resilience (ISO 22316), risk management standards (ISO 31000) including risk management in supply chains (PAS 7000), environmental management standards (ISO 14001), business continuity (ISO 22301), and quality and satisfaction management client (ISO 9001). Research in 2018 was conducted on a sample of 808 enterprises located in Australia, China, India, Japan, Great Britain, Ireland, and the USA, of which 52% recorded revenues of over USD 500 million in the previous year (BSI, 2018).

The same framework was implemented a few years later in the annual research by BSI to recognize the effects of COVID-19. In 2021, BSI interviewed more than 500 business leaders all over the world to learn how they survived, stabilized, rebuilt, and thrived after the pandemic. The results of the research stressed lessons learned, i.e.:

■ Holistic approach is the key, as all aspects of operations impact organizational resilience,
■ Agility supported by people and processes gains importance in the context of organizational resilience,
■ Recognizing and appreciating the health, safety, and wellbeing of employees and communities helps to rebuild organizational resilience,
■ Flexibility and adaptability result in recovery opportunities and resilience.

The model presented is universal; it does not refer to any specific industry, sector, or company size; however, it receives some criticism. Holden et al. (2016) implement the BS standard, which includes a basic model of organizational resilience based on 24 questions divided into 6 sections. However, the questions can only lead to a subjective, qualitative assessment of the organization's resilience. A quantitative approach to assessing organizational resilience, is not defined in the standard. Hence, the following steps are suggested:

■ Update the enterprise risk register to include the concept of resilience.
■ Quantify the cost and effort that would be required to restore balance after a disruption (i.e., one of the entries in the risk register).
■ Relate work inputs and the risk register to company resources.
■ Define indicators that can assess organizational resilience attributes.

The suggestions are quite general yet can be operationalized to make a universal comparison of the level of organizational resilience of various companies.

An example of a disturbance-oriented resilience model is the one developed by Tierney (2003) in the context of the September 11, 2001, attack on the World Trade Center. According to the author, organizational resilience is characterized by:

- robustness;
- redundancy and interchangeability may also refer to fully replaceable reserves or security resources;
- entrepreneurship, resourcefulness;
- speed, quickness.

The author also points to four interdependent dimensions that can characterize the resilience of an organization:

- Technical dimension – that is, according to the author, the ability of physical systems to work at the assumed level, despite the occurrence of a disruption.
- Organizational dimension – according to the author, it is the ability to make decisions and take actions to reduce the negative effects of a disruption.
- Social dimension – i.e., the ability to minimize negative social and communication effects.
- Economic dimension – is the ability to minimize direct and indirect financial losses related to the disruption.

Based on the research conducted and reports available after the attack, the author assesses the activities related to mitigating the effects as resilient. Tierney focuses on the event and the organizations, businesses, and communities that were involved in rescue and prevention actions. It is the set of independent organizations and the chains that were created between them during the attack that he assesses as the leading feature of the organization's resilience.

1.3.2.2 Organizational Resilience Model

Organizational resilience can be assessed from the perspective of employees (individuals) or from the perspective of the organization. An example of assessing organizational resilience from an individual perspective is the one by Mallak (1998), where organizational resilience is defined as the ability of an individual or organization to continuously design and implement positive adaptive processes that function in accordance with sudden events (i.e., crises) while maintaining minimal effort or stress for the organization. In order to assess the resilience of an organization, Mallak defines three dimensions of resilience assessment, based on Weick's (1996) concept. These are:

- Bricolage – the ability to improvise in an organization, benefit from creativity under pressure, and act in chaotic conditions, trying to put them in order.
- Attitude of wisdom – wisdom of using past experiences with skepticism on the one hand and curiosity on the other, using many sources of information.
- Virtual role systems (VRS), which refer to advanced forms of team relationships.

Based on the research conducted, the author defined 6 factors that can be used to assess the level of an organization's resilience:

- Goal-directed solution-seeking – a factor corresponding to the need for vision and goals to build creativity in the process of searching for solutions to problems.
- Avoidance – strongly correlated with the previously defined term Bricolage.
- Critical understanding – can be understood as awareness of the problems and priorities that result from the crisis.
- Role dependence – identified with a previously defined virtual role system (VRS).
- Source reliance – involves using several sources of information, which leads to building reality based on richer data. These sources should be selected wisely and the information balanced.
- Resource access – to solve a given problem, you need access to resources or the ability to access them despite the difficulties encountered.

The above factors were indicated as the most important in assessing an organization's resilience, but Mallak does not present a specific scale or questions that could be implemented in an organization.

The approach to organizational model and assessment using organization's perspective is the one presented in the research by Chen et al. (2021).

They developed their approach based on selected cases of resilient companies. Case studies used available information and open coding procedure to interpret collected data, and the meaning behind them. The used collated information for conceptualization and further categorization giving the following categories, somehow describing resilient companies: capital structure, cash storage, debt service, debt service capacity, product features, operation strategy, price conflict, survival crisis, emotional connection, reciprocal relationship, customer service, relationship enhancement, employee commitment, spiritual shaping, rigid and flexible, community sense, emotional regulation, positive awareness, behavioral characteristics, and learning capabilities.

The next was axial coding, linking the categories by assigning them to a logically defined causal line following the structure: causal conditions, phenomena, action strategy, results. Products of axial coding were the main categories: capital resilience, strategic resilience, cultural resilience, relationship resilience, and learning resilience. These are the core categories contributing to resilience, also referred to as resilience dimensions. Chen et al. (2021) also present an approach to resilience assessment. They complement each dimension with a brief definition and develop it into descriptive scale items that are statements a company should refer to when being assessed.

The capital resilience is defined as the ability of a business to operate normally and to recapitalize against risk in a crisis. It is decomposed into the following scale items:

- Our business has a good cash flow;
- We will base our cash reserves on our corporate strategy and competitive model;
- We have a solid capital structure;
- We have a multiple sources of financing;
- We have a low capital leverage;
- We will make profit maximization the ultimate goal of our business;
- We have high capital utilization efficiency.

Strategic resilience is defined as the ability to maintain strategic consistency over time, helping them to identify and eliminate disadvantages and to be able to choose the right growth model. It is decomposed into the following scale items:

- Our company is able to focus on its core business;
- Our company is able to identify unfavorable factors in development in a timely manner;

- We pursue a robust strategic growth model;
- We were able to clarify our strategic positioning;
- We are able to match strategic objectives and operational capabilities very well.

Cultural resilience is defined via corporate culture, which shapes the entrepreneurial spirit of employees and their commitment to the organization and is decomposed into the following scale items:

- Our corporate culture is designed to foster a sense of community among our employees;
- Our corporate culture fosters a sense of cooperation among our employees;
- Our corporate culture inspires employee morale and spirit;
- Our corporate culture reflects the care and love we have for our employees;
- Our corporate culture fosters a sense of organizational commitment.

Relationship resilience is defined as a reciprocal relationship between business and stakeholders and decomposed into the following scale items:

- We create a unique value for our customers;
- We are able to think about our customers;
- We aim for shared prosperity between companies and stakeholders;
- We have a good reciprocal relationship with our investors;
- We are able to fully listen to the advice of our investors.

Learning resilience is defined as the ability of companies to cope with the pressures and challenges of learning and is decomposed into the following scale items:

- We will choose the learning target according to the characteristics of our own company;
- We will choose the better companies to study;
- We will have a deep awareness of our situation in time;
- We will make timely adjustments to our positioning;
- We will be interested in adjusting our emotions to get into the study state more quickly.

The scales presented are universal in terms of business and company size. They should be implemented by presenting them to managers representing various areas of a company to provide a complete and holistic view and enable resilience measurement.

A dimension of environment in resilience assessment was added by Burnard et al. (2018). They focused on organizations that experienced major disruptions and operated at a high level of risk resulting from the difficult organizational environment. They identified disruptions relevant to the organization, including: delayed deliveries, loss of key staff, equipment failures, and changes in legislation, and defined two dimensions of organizational resilience:

■ preparation;
■ adaptation.

With respect to the above dimensions, the authors defined four organizational configurations:

■ resourceful;
■ at high risk;
■ process based;
■ resilience focused.

The authors focused on comparing the condition of an organization before and during the disruption, not taking recovery after a disruption into consideration.

1.3.2.3   Resilience in Industry 4.0

Industry 4.0 is, on the one hand, a contemporary manufacturing management paradigm, and on the other, a set of tools and methods manufacturing companies implement to become more competitive. Morisse and Prigge (2017) link Industry 4.0 with resilience in their framework for evaluating Resilience in Industry 4.0. The starting point in their model is the architecture of Industry 4.0, which includes four pillars, namely people, technologies, processes, and information, with:

■ Characteristics of resilience: flexibility, efficiency, cohesion, adaptability, and diversity;

- Strategies for resilience: discovering, avoiding, doing nothing, reducing, and managing;
- Phases of resilience: readiness, response, and recovery.

The links identified explain the path towards resilience:

- Pillar 1: people – they have the knowledge, skills, and attitude enabling the detection of a problem and the response to disruptive events. They are a key resource in a crisis situation, and they should be prepared (with proper training) to detect, respond, and recover from threats.
- Pillar 2: process – processes determine performance, and they should be continuously improved to benefit from developing technologies. Industry 4.0 offers numerous technologies supporting efficient data flow, shortening production cycles, minimizing cost and improving quality.
- Pillar 3: technology – processes should be equipped with proper technologies to be more efficient. Industry 4.0 is a set of technologies such as autonomous robots, additive printing, big data, and many others that provide the capability to respond to disruptions and recover – bringing manufacturing processes to their regular performance.
- Pillar 4: information – dealing with an excessive amount of data and collecting and processing data valuable for a company supports reactive and effective management and decision-making. Industry 4.0 benefits from big data and cloud computing technologies, enabling the most efficient response to disruptions possible.

The pillars should be implemented to provide diversity of solutions/options, flexibility, efficiency, cohesion, and adaptability, and result in the resilience of the enterprise.

1.3.2.4   On-Line Resilience Assessment

Over time, benefiting from the development of the Internet, its openness, and its impact range, some online resilience assessment tools were developed. One of the examples is OrgRes Tool (Organizational Resilience Tool, https://www.resorgs.org.nz/orgres-tool/). It is a free diagnostic form available online. It offers a comprehensive assessment of an organization's resilience based on 13 questions. Each question refers to a different indicator defined by experts appointed by the New Zealand government in cooperation with REAG (Resilient Expert Advisory Group) and the Resilient Organization from New Zealand.

The survey involves a subjective assessment of the weakness and strength of a given value on a scale from 0 to 7 (0 is for "I am not sure", 1 is the weakest, and 7 is the strongest). The values taken into account in the form are:

- leadership skills;
- employee engagement;
- understanding the current situation of the organization (situation awareness);
- decision-making ability;
- innovation and creativity;
- effective partnership;
- even distribution of knowledge (leveraging knowledge);
- ability to cooperate (breaking silos);
- appropriate level of internal resources – human resources;
- unity and agreement of purpose;
- proactive posture;
- planning strategies;
- strength testing – analysis of weaknesses and vulnerabilities (stress testing plan).

Complementary information indicates whether a given organization belongs to a higher-risk sector and what the size of the organization is. The result of the above survey is sent to the user by e-mail, in graphical form, along with a comprehensive interpretation in descriptive form.

The assessment presented above is quite simple; however, there are also examples of more complex online resilience assessments. One of them is Organizational resilience HealthCheck which is based on the OrgRes Tool but more detailed (https://www.cisc.gov.au/how-we-support-industry/organisational-resilience/organisational-resilience-healthcheck-tool). It assesses and rates organizations across 13 resilience indicators (similar to the OrgRes Tool), including:

1. Leadership
2. Decision-Making
3. Situational Awareness
4. Creativity and Innovation
5. Employee Engagement
6. Collaboration
7. Resource Management
8. Knowledge Management

9. Silo Mentality
10. Exercise Management
11. Foresight
12. Unity of Purpose
13. Proactive Posture

Each of the 13 above-mentioned categories corresponds to specific features assessed on a scale from 1 to 4. Based on the answers, a score is assigned, which, after the final summary, indicates the strength of the organization's resilience. In addition, for each category, there is a short summary of possible actions to strengthen the strength of a given feature and potential factors that block the organization from strengthening its resilience. The questionnaire defined a total of 64 features assigned to them, which were divided into three main groups:

■ leadership and organizational culture,
■ networks and relationships,
■ readiness for change.

On this basis, an organization can obtain a maximum of 256 points. The first survey conducted should indicate the baseline state of the organization's resilience. Based on it, the company can identify the weak points of a given team or company and work on improving them. The effects can be verified by repeating the survey.

This HealthCheck Tool was first developed in 2015. The University of Tasmania, with support from the REAG, comprehensively updated the tool between 2023 and 2024. This ensures it has the latest contemporary methodologies for enhancing organizational resilience.

Updating the HealthCheck Tool is a key initiative of the Australian Government's 2023 Critical Infrastructure Resilience Strategy.

1.3.2.5 Relative Overall Resilience (ROR)

The Relative Overall Resilience model by McManus et al. (2008) is based on three factors: situation awareness, management of keystone vulnerabilities, and adaptive capacity. These factors were decomposed into five indicators and operationalized as 49 statements in a survey tool.

■ Situation awareness is decomposed into: roles and responsibilities, understanding and analysis of hazards and consequences, connectivity awareness, insurance awareness, and recovery priorities.

■ Management of keystone vulnerabilities is decomposed into: planning strategies, participation in exercises, capability and capacity of internal resources, capability and capacity of external resources, and organizational connectivity.

■ Adaptive capacity is decomposed into: silo mentality, communications and relationships, strategic vision and outcome expectancy, information and knowledge, leadership, and management and governance structures.

The statements in the survey tool refer to each indicator describing the organization's features in terms of resilience. The sentences are presented to people of the organization. The respondents should represent all levels and functions of organization. Multiple responses provide a broader and deeper understanding of organizational resilience and the plans, procedures, and strategies embedded in its culture.

McManus' approach was reviewed by Lee and Kotler (2011). Their research led to retaining 37 items and simplifying the assessment. The model of Adjusted ROR adds one factor to organizational resilience, namely resilience ethos. The resilience ethos factor is measured using two indicators: commitment to resilience and a network perspective, while the other three factors are measured using seven indicators each. Compared to the lists presented above, the following changes were introduced:

■ Indicators added to the situational awareness scope: include internal and external situation monitoring and reporting, informed decision making.

■ Indicators added to the management of keystone vulnerabilities scope: include robust processes for identifying and analyzing vulnerabilities and staff engagement and involvement.

■ Indicators added to the adaptive capacity scope: include innovation and creativity, devolved and responsive decision-making.

This model was operationalized as 73 items, yet 57 of them were retained as the most important. The research conducted proved that there were two crucial and two weak factors, and 53 indicators were recognized as important.

1.3.2.6 Resilience Analysis Grid (RAG)

The Resilience Analysis Grid (RAG) was developed by Hollnagel (2014). The model is based on four abilities that are necessary for resilient performance (Hollnagel, 2014):

- The ability to respond, which is based on knowing what to do, or being able to respond to regular and irregular changes, disturbances, and opportunities by activating prepared actions or by adjusting the current mode of functioning.
- The ability to monitor is based on knowing what to look for, or being able to monitor that which is or could seriously affect the system's performance in the near term – positively or negatively. The monitoring must cover the system's own performance as well as what happens in the environment.
- The ability to learn, which is based on knowing what has happened or being able to learn from experience, in particular to learn the right lessons from the right experience, corresponds with the double-loop learning concept.
- The ability to anticipate is based on knowing what to expect or being able to anticipate developments further into the future, such as potential disruptions, novel demands or constraints, new opportunities, or changing operating conditions.

The abilities are decomposed into specific issues describing organizational behavior. The process of assessment is open, and the issues are not pre-defined. The procedure of assessment is defined as a four-phase process:

- The first phase is the definition and description of the system structure, constraints, time horizon, and resources involved in the structures.
- In the second phase, appropriate questions are selected that correspond to the analyzed system or organization.
- In the third phase, selected questions are assessed for each of the above-mentioned four characteristics.
- In the fourth phase, the results should be combined, and the answers obtained should be shared.

The issues identified in the second stage are rated in the third stage, and a Likert-type scale can be used (however, it is a suggestion and not a requirement):

■ Excellent – the system meets and exceeds the criteria for the required ability.
■ Satisfactory – the system fully meets all reasonable criteria for the required ability.
■ Acceptable – the system meets the nominal criteria for the required ability.
■ Unacceptable – the system does not meet the nominal criteria for the required ability.
■ Deficient – there is insufficient ability to provide the required ability.
■ Missing – there is no ability to provide the required ability.

Another approach to assessment is presented by Patriarca et al. (2018). They define organizational resilience as:

■ ability to react to any event;
■ ability to monitor ongoing evolutions;
■ ability to anticipate threats and opportunities;
■ the ability to draw conclusions and learn from past events.

and suggest adding the AHP (Analytical Hierarchy Process) hierarchical method to the assessment. AHP was first presented by Saaty (2004) and involves four steps:

■ Create a hierarchical structure for the decision-making process.
■ Define the decision-maker's preferences and calculate his preferences for all elements of the hierarchy.
■ Examine the consistency of the constructed preference matrix.
■ Create the final ranking.

The procedure is flexible and universal because of the openness of the issues list and measurement methodology.

1.3.3 Conclusion

Resilience is an interesting concept in management field; moreover, it is a universal term that can be referred to any organizations. Its importance is greater, the more disturbances appear, the more frequent they are, and the longer they last. The contemporary world exposes individuals and organizations to numerous disturbances, hazards, and threats. Generally, they are perceived negatively, yet in some cases they contribute to renewal, discovering new opportunities, and development thanks to organizational resilience. Based on the structure of contemporary markets and management the following domains of organizational resilience are identified (BSI): operational resilience, supply chain resilience, information resilience, and the following essential elements are recognized (BSI): product excellence, process reliability, and people behaviors. The value added in research on resilience is recognizing the response patterns and analyzing recovery processes so they can be disseminated as best practices and contribute to the better performance of various organizations. A resilient organization benefits from (BSI):

■ Strategic adaptability – giving them the ability to handle changing circumstances successfully, even if this means moving away from their core business.
■ Agile leadership – allowing them to take measured risks with confidence and respond quickly and appropriately to both opportunity and threat.
■ Robust governance –demonstrating accountability across organizational structures, based upon a culture of trust, transparency and innovation, ensuring they remain true to their vision and values.

The expected benefits are attractive, hence the number and scope of research in the field. The models presented in the chapter are interrelated as the authors review each other's work and benefit from the experience and findings of other researchers.

1.4 Readiness, Maturity, and Resilience

The term "maturity" is related to the term "readiness", but they do have different meanings. They are relative and related (DeCarolis et al., 2017).

Maturity is a state that enables gradual, continuous improvement (Mittal et al., 2018). Readiness assessment involves analyzing and determining the level of preparedness, attitudes, and resources at all levels of the system (Mittal et al., 2018). Readiness explains whether an organization is ready to start the development process or not (Akdil et al., 2018).

It is important to distinguish the concepts of "maturity" and "readiness". Schumacher et al. (2016) express the difference between these two concepts by prioritizing readiness before the initiation of the maturation process. This means that a readiness assessment takes place before engaging in the maturation process. Maturity assessment, on the other hand, aims to capture the state as it is during the maturation process. While readiness shows whether the organization is ready to start the development process, maturity shows the level of development in terms of improving the area of operation. So, readiness is "the willingness or state of being prepared to do something" (Oxford, 2010), and maturity is "a very advanced or developed form or state" (Oxford, 2010).

The issue of "maturity" and "readiness" and their importance in systems engineering decision-making has come into sharp focus with the increased interest in recent years in the ability to assess "metrics" such as "Technology Readiness Levels" (TRL) (e.g. Mankis, 1995), "System Readiness Levels" (SRL), "Integration Readiness Levels" (IRL) (e.g. Gove, 2008), and "Manufacturing Readiness Levels" (MRL). Research (Kober and Sauser, 2008; Sauser, et al., 2006, 2008) also revealed the difficulty of achieving meaningful, clear, and measurable indicators. One aspect of this difficulty arises from the fact that the concepts of "maturity" and "readiness" only have full meaning in the context of "mature enough for what?" and "ready for what?" (Tetlay and John, 2009).

Tetlay and John, in their research, consider whether there is a sufficiently clear distinction between "System Maturity" (SM) and "System Readiness" (SR) (Tetlay and John, 2009). According to them, current definitions of readiness seem to assess SM to determine SR (Tetlay and John, 2009). According to Tetlay and John, the concept of "maturity" is included in the concept of "readiness" (Tetlay and John, 2009). Therefore, in research, they are not considered as two distinct and separate concepts and are not used in isolation but interchangeably. Maturity is therefore considered a part of readiness, and one cannot talk about readiness without discussing or mentioning maturity, and vice versa. Readiness and maturity are not mutually exclusive. It could be argued that existing readiness levels actually provide a "maturity" metric as opposed to a "readiness" metric. According to Dowling and Pardoe, "readiness" values are typically soft measures that are relatively easy to calculate but require supporting justification that explains the assessment and the averaged ambiguities (Dowling and Pardoe, 2005).

The term "maturity" is also associated with the concept of "resilience", a mature system is often considered a resilient system; however, these concepts are not equivalent. Resilience is defined as the ability to anticipate, prepare for, respond to, and adapt to increasing change and unexpected disruptions in order to survive and thrive (Ambulkar et al., 2015). Resilience is a feature of an organization that enables its survival and sustainable development, built on the one hand by the organization's lack of susceptibility to the impact of crisis factors, enabling the avoidance of problems and difficulties, and, on the other hand, the ability to resist the impact of these factors (i.e. the organization's ability to respond) and, on the other hand, their occurrence, regardless of where they are located (external, internal), i.e. the ability of the organization to maintain its integrity (survive) and operate correctly (satisfactory) during the impact of crisis factors, i.e. the state of the organization conditioned by the overall management processes in order to restore the integrity of its environment internal (i.e. ensuring its durability and sustainable development), destroyed by crisis factors (Bhamra et al., 2011). A resilient organization is therefore one that demonstrates "long-term development capacity and good economic condition that is maintained despite changes in external conditions" (Brusset and Teller, 2017).

Relations between readiness, maturity, and resilience were inspiration to develop an integrated contemporary management model referring to those terms. The model is operationalized to enable the diagnosis of a company via readiness/maturity/resilience assessment, and to support continuous improvement by suggesting strategies for further development.

Chapter 2

Management Excellence Model

2.1 Exogenous Approach to Changes

In the context of social sciences, especially management, which is a relatively young discipline, changes occur frequently, which results from the fact that these sciences are largely conditioned by civilizational, cultural (Pietruszka-Ortyl, 2012), economic and social factors, characterized by significant dynamics. In the modern world, a key phenomenon is progressive globalization (Mazurkiewicz, 2011), which concerns all areas of human activity, including its functioning as an individual, but also the functioning of entire societies. The consequences of globalization can be observed at the product level and include:

- shortening the product life cycle on the market,
- possibilities of extending the product life cycle in slower-growing markets,
- striving for rapid product development,
- complementary (thanks to modularization) trends in product standardization and customization.

And at the process level, they include:

- fast pace of development of new technologies and operating techniques,

DOI: 10.4324/9781032688404-2

- fast pace of implementation of new techniques and technologies,
- pressure to reduce costs.

Whereas at the organizational level, they are observed in the form of:

- creation of new organizational forms (supply chains and networks),
- internal and external integration,
- customer orientation (focus on customer needs),
- efficiency orientation (input-result relationship).

While and at the market level, they manifest themselves with:

- the disappearance of many existing markets and the emergence of new ones,
- intensifying competition,
- internationalization of enterprises.

Some of the phenomena mentioned have already occurred in the economy, but to a smaller extent and with less intensity. Currently, what is characteristic is their simultaneous, parallel occurrence, and the growing scope, pace of spread and relationships between them (interactions are most often positive, because changes occurring in one area not only initiate but also strengthen changes in other, related areas). With this in mind, Ansoff defined four tendencies observed in contemporary world and including (Ansoff, 1985):

- an increase in the novelty of changes, changes are more and more often discontinued, therefore previous experiences become less and less useful,
- an increase in the intensity of the environment, understood as the sum of energy that group members devote to interacting with others,
- increasing the speed of changes in the environment, i.e. shortening the cycle from technology development to its commercialization,
- increasing complexity of the environment.

After almost 40 years, his observations proved to be right. These trends, occurring together, contribute to the phenomenon known as turbulence, which characterizes the modern environment.

The growing interest in the phenomenon and its inclusion in publications results in the spread of the approach and its increasing importance. Due to the number and diversity of areas affected by turbulence and the consequences it causes on a global scale and scope, the turbulence postulate is treated as a meta-paradigm (Krupski, 2013). The examples of turbulences in contemporary world include phenomena that cut across political, economic, social, environmental, and technological dimensions, moreover, they often intersect, creating complex and multifaceted issues. Dealing with these turbulences requires effective governance, cooperation, and resilience at local, national, and international levels. In many cases dealing with turbulences is basically mitigating their effects and decreasing probability of turbulences occurrence, however, in some cases turbulences may result in positive changes, development and innovation. Hence, in general, recognition of turbulences and their patterns is the most important and should be followed by addressing underlying systemic issues, promoting sustainable development, fostering innovation, and strengthening multilateral cooperation. The expected outcome is building a more stable, equitable, and resilient companies, economy and society in the face of contemporary challenges. The most often mentioned turbulences in the last 20 years include:

- Geopolitical tensions and conflicts (Caldara and Iacoviello, 2022) continue to pose significant challenges to global stability. Because of international/global nature of economies and supply chains conflicts are no longer local as they impact companies creating interconnected networks cooperating to manufacture and deliver products worldwide. Issues such as territorial disputes, power struggles, terrorism, and regional conflicts contribute to geopolitical turbulence and many examples are being observed on the global arena.
- Geopolitical crises (Raikes et al., 2022) may cause increased migration flows, humanitarian challenges and refugee crises driven by intercultural conflict, poverty, and socio-economic disparities.
- To deal with social turbulences emerging from migration and humanitarian challenges political initiatives are undertaken (Lin, 2023), some of them leading to balancing the situation and some striving for imbalance and deepened polarization, based on populism, and identity-based conflicts within societies. The latter contribute to social turbulences spreading unrest, political instability, and challenges to democratic governance.
- Interconnectivity of economies (Wong and Fong, 2011) contributes to welfare spreading on hand but on the other enables propagation of crises on a global scale. Economic instability, including factors such as

trade disputes, financial crises, income inequality, and global economic slowdowns, creates uncertainty for businesses, governments, and individuals alike. Since business all over the world cooperate economic difficulties in one of the network nods can easily impact the others.

■ Industry 4.0/Industry 5.0 (Xu et al., 2021) as a general term referring to the rapid technological advancements. Technological advancement itself is a positive phenomenon, however, it creates the need to adjust company's resources, both technical and human, which is cost and time consuming as investments need to made and followed by training to adjust infrastructure and skills profiles. Turbulences in that case are disruptive changes in companies and supply chains that lead to improved performance yet expose companies to threats such as cybersecurity and ethical concerns connected with advanced technology use (artificial intelligence and biotechnology are the examples of concerns most often raised).

■ Cybersecurity (Craigen et al., 2014) is also considered a turbulence as it may disturb supply chains, pose risk to critical infrastructure, businesses, governments, and individuals. The consequences are of social, political and economic nature.

■ One of consequences of global economy and technology development (Weaver et al., 2017), followed by worldwide consumption increase is climate change caused by pollution. The phenomenon is was recognized in the 90s of 20th century and the initiatives were taken to counteract, yet the consequences of industry development and civilization growth are strongly impacting societies. Severe temperatures, storms, winds disturb not only everyday life but also business operations and socio-economic stability. Ecosystems suffer from pollution, natural disasters and decreased bio-diversity.

■ Climate changes (Ucal and Xydis, 2020) result in decreased biodiversity and availability of resources, which relates to both, non-renewable resources and renewable resources as their availability may be reduced in a given period of time due to the renewal period. Resource scarcity results in competition for natural resources, including water, energy, and minerals. Competition exacerbates geopolitical tensions and may lead to environmental degradation, particularly in regions prone to natural resource scarcity and without means to protect their resources.

■ The turbulence impacting societies and economies on a global scale and in the long time span, was undoubtedly Covid-19 pandemic (Clemente-Suárez et al., 2021). Economic downturns and decreased consumer spending during the pandemic (caused by fear of job loss and uncertainty of future, especially in the early stages of pandemic development) resulted in revenue losses for many companies, particularly those in the travel, hospitality, and retail sectors. Businesses faced cash flow challenges, reduced profitability, and increased debt burdens, leading to layoffs, furloughs, and bankruptcies. Pandemic was devastating for life and health of many, disturbed and deconstructed healthcare systems all over the world, disrupted supply chains and stopped economies worldwide for many weeks. Pandemic has changed management paradigms, shifting the back to inventory keeping local (or at least diversified) supply chains; education systems, making them more flexible and in many cases more accessible thanks to remote teaching tools; societies, making them more health aware but also causing many psychological problems emerging from isolation and stress caused by persistent exposure to life threat. The consequences of Covid-19 were discussed in many contexts and perspectives. The most often mentioned include supply chain disruptions caused by lockdowns, travel restrictions, and factory closures and leading to shortages of raw materials, components, and finished goods. Companies representing many industries all over the world faced delays in production and distribution, and customers faced shortages in many products, starting for everyday products but also reaching electronics and all the products equipped with electronic components. Lockdowns changed business operations and forced companies to rethink their business models. The need to keep hygienic standards and social distancing measures opened new opportunities for work organization. Many companies had to rapidly implement remote work arrangements. While this enabled business continuity, it also presented challenges in terms of maintaining productivity, communication, and employee well-being. However, after pandemics, remote work gained its acceptance and many companies continue work in remote and hybrid mode. Remote work implementation was possible thanks to digital transformation, it is believed that the pandemic accelerated digital transformation initiatives as companies adapted to remote operations and shifted to online sales and services. Organizations invested in e-commerce platforms, digital collaboration tools, and automation technologies to enhance resilience and agility in the face of disruptions. They had to reassess their business models and strategies to align with changing environment constraints, consumer preferences, market dynamics, and regulatory requirements. Companies in industries such as healthcare, education, and entertainment identified demand for remote services and digital solutions as an opportunity. New solutions such as telemedicine, online learning platforms, streaming services, and virtual events were developed as consumers sought alternatives to in-person activities. Many businesses diversified their product offerings, expanded digital channels, and prioritized health and safety measures to adapt to the so called new normal. Employers implemented measures such as previously mentioned remote work policies, physical distancing protocols, enhanced cleaning and sanitizing procedures, and personal protective equipment (PPE) requirements. Ensuring a safe work environment became a top priority for companies.

Generally the consequence of pandemic was growing interest in resilience, from both individual perspective, in health context, and in business perspective. The pandemic and the impact it had on economy initiated the need for building resilient and agile supply chains capable of responding to disruptions. Companies reevaluated their supply chain strategies, diversified sourcing, and implemented risk management measures to mitigate future disruptions. Decision makers understood that they should be aware of unpredictability of the world and disruptions that may happen.

Overall, the Covid-19 pandemic has reshaped the business and economy, prompting companies to adapt to new realities, embrace digital innovation, and prioritize resilience and flexibility in their operations and strategies. The long-term consequences of the pandemic are likely to continue influencing business practices and industry dynamics for years to come.

2.1.1 Turbulence in an Organization's Environment

The enterprise's environment is an important element of any organizational model; its inclusion results from the widely accepted systemic approach to organization, according to which the organization as an open system operates in the environment with which it interacts and exchanges information, materials, and energy (Forrester, 1968).

The environment can be defined as the totality of conditions and interdependencies of various elements (including other organizations), spheres, phenomena, processes, and trends that are not part of the organizational system under consideration and remain beyond its direct control but are related to it, i.e., they exert an influence on a given organization and/or are influenced by the behavior, actions, and decisions, management processes, structural solutions, and development prospects of a given organization (Matejun and Nowicki, 2013).

In the literature, you can find a number of criteria characterizing the environment, which are also used to classify it. Examples of these are presented in Table 2.1. The presented criteria are ordered from those relating to the structure of the environment, the most static, to those characterizing the behavior of the environment, the most dynamic.

The characteristics and classifications of the environment presented in the table refer to specific criteria; however, the description and characteristics of the environment can also be presented in a synthetic way, taking

Table 2.1 Examples of Environmental Classification

Criterion	Characteristics	Classification
Reality	Analysis of the environment in relation to socio-economic reality	1. Real 2. E-environment 3. Simulated
Time	Analysis of the environment in relation to the current period. The time criterion determines the order of events and the intervals between events occurring in the surrounding space.	1. Past (historical) 2. Present 3. Future
Complexity	Analysis of the environment in terms of number, complexity, and diversity elements present in it. Interconnections and relationships between individual elements, dimensions, and planes of the environment also become an important dimension of this feature.	1. Simple 2. Complex
Space	Analysis of the environment from a physical point of view, extent considered in context, geographical and administrative. These characteristics are related to the presence of specific elements and trends as well as the course of various phenomena and processes within a specific environment.	1. Local 2. Regional 3. Domestic 4. International 5. Global

(Continued)

Table 2.1 (*Continued*)   Examples of Environmental Classification

Criterion	Characteristics	Classification
Focus	Analysis of the environment, which involves the presence of certain conditions in the environment elements, spheres, phenomena, processes, trends, and their mutual connections and dependencies. This feature is complemented by the level, distance, and direction of interactions between the organizational system and its external environment.	1. Closer 2. Further
Predictability	Analysis of the environment in terms of opportunities anticipating and forecasting changes and developments in them.	1. Possible to predict based on statistical tools 2. Predictable based on qualitative methods 3. Impossible to predict
Plasticity	Analysis of the environment from the point of view of the organization's ability to influence its elements, processes and phenomena.	1. Easy to shape 2. Difficult to shape 3. Impossible to shape
Attitude	Analysis of the environment from a point of view of the attitude of its elements and spheres to the functioning of the organization	1. Positive (supporting) 2. Neutral 3. Hostile
Capacity	Analysis of the environment in terms of its ability to create opportunities for the organization to continue, develop and grow.	1. High capacity 2. Low capacity
Reactiveness	Analysis of the environment in terms of its reactions (impact) on activities undertaken by organizations.	1. Reactive 2. Passive
Changeability	Analyzing the environment for speed and the dynamics of changes taking place and their strength and the intensity of the impact of these changes on organizations.	1. Stable 2. Changing 3. Turbulent 4. Twinkling

Source: With changes (Matejun, 2016).

into account the interdependencies between the criteria (Wach, 1998). The following dimensions and features can be taken into account synthetically (Bluedorn, 1993):

■ dynamics,
■ uncertainty,
■ complexity,
■ munificence.

The mentioned characteristics of the environment are interdependent and condition each other. Dynamics reflects the degree of instability of the basic elements of the environment (Scharfman and Dean, 1991), resulting from the arrangement and characteristics of external factors leading to changes that are impossible to predict and plan by the company's management (Aldrich, 1979). The decreasing predictability of changes (uncertainty) in the environment (Ansoff, 1985) seems to be a tendency commonly recognized and taken into account in the context of decision-making determinants. The scope, intensity, and depth of changes (generosity) in the characteristics of the environment (Bednarczyk, 1996) determine the dynamics of changes and allow us to determine the type of environment. In turn, the greater the complexity, the more numerous and more complicated are the connections between the elements of the organizational system, and, consequently, the more difficult it is to identify and manage the cause-and-effect relationships constituting the essence of changes, and the greater the scope of these changes. If the environment is stable and simple, it is characterized by low uncertainty: a few similar external factors, factors that are constant or change little; if it is complex, it is characterized by moderately low uncertainty: a large number of external factors that are similar to each other, factors that are constant or change little. On the other hand, if the environment is unstable and simple, it is characterized by moderately high uncertainty: few similar external factors, factors change frequently and unpredictably, whereas if it is complex, it is characterized by high uncertainty: few similar external factors, factors change frequently and unpredictably (Brews and Purohit, 2007).

The uncertainty scale is based on two factors: the complexity of the environment (a distinction is made between simple and complex) and its dynamics (a distinction is made between stable and unstable), which results in four levels of environmental uncertainty. Four levels of variability are also identified by Matejun (Matejun, 2016), distinguishing between stable, variable, turbulent, and flickering environments. In a shimmering environment, the variability is so great that opportunities for enterprises appear suddenly and last for a short time, and their use significantly determines the market position of the organization and allows for the quick achievement of a significant competitive advantage.

Other classifications presented in the literature refer to a stable, variable, or turbulent environment (Stoner and Wankel, 1997) (in a trichotomous approach), or in the polarized version, a stable and turbulent environment (Ansoff, 1985) (dichotomous approach).

A stable environment enables enterprises to function in a repetitive manner, based on forecasting and planning. The variable environment is characterized by an average level of scope, intensity, and depth (degree of enterprise penetration) of changes, therefore a market situation that is subject to fluctuations, but to some extent predictable. Enterprises are able to proactively adapt to changes in the environment as long as they are flexible. In turn, a turbulent environment is characterized by such dynamics of changes that make it impossible to anticipate them and therefore make the company unable to react to them.

The levels of environmental variability (in the most common, trichotomous approach) and the characteristics associated with them, related to the analytical approach, characteristics of the environment, and main areas of the organization, are summarized in Table 2.2.

A turbulent environment characterized by the most intense changes is referred to in the literature as a turbulent environment. Definitions of turbulence presented in the literature are usually based on Ansoff's concept, not negating but only complementing and extending his concept. The list of selected turbulence definitions is presented in Table 2.3.

Turbulence is therefore variability that poses challenges to the company, variability resulting from the behavior of customers, competitors, and environmental conditions, difficult (impossible?) to model, occurring on a macroscale (globally, regionally, within the country) and microscale (in a single industry or company) (Kotler and Armstrong, 2011).

Ansoff indicates the sources of turbulence in his definition, giving trends in the modern economy that contribute to their creation. However, there is a view in the literature that environmental turbulence is not a universal feature and applies only to certain industries or environments. It results from changes in political and economic systems (and therefore the characteristics of the macro-environment) or the specificity of the industry (technology, innovation, connections with science and research and development)

Table 2.2 Characteristics of Environmental Types

Characteristics	Stable Environment	Changing Environment	Turbulent Environment
Analytic approach	Synchronous analysis	Systemic analysis	Diachronic analysis
Emphatic factor	Internal elements in the organization, compliance of processes occurring in the organization and the environment	Interdependence of the organization and the environment, managerial decisions made in connection with changes in the environment	The dynamics of the environment and changes in the environment are more important than the rules of operation within the organization
Market driving forces	Stable market needs (balance between supply and demand), stable competition, and a relatively constant number of customers	Changeable market situation, moderate competition, predictable, new competitors appear, current ones withdraw	High variability of market needs, fierce competition, market situation difficult to predict
Technical driving forces	None or slight changes in technology; changes that do not result in improving parameters of products; few and non-revolutionary changes that do not bring a breakthrough in values utility products and methods of production and distribution	increasing pace of change in technology; changes affecting the quality of products and methods of using production factors; innovations with a growing tendency to be incremental, non-revolutionary, and predictable	high pace of creation and application of technical progress; rapid obsolescence of technology and products; big, frequency of discoveries and inventions varies over time

(Continued)

Table 2.2 (*Continued*)   Characteristics of Environmental Types

Characteristics	*Stable Environment*	*Changing Environment*	*Turbulent Environment*
Social and political driving forces	Sociopolitical peace	uncertainty without signs of unrest; symptoms of social discouragement	rapid socio-political changes; high tensions in the country and/or internationally; significant disruptions in legislation
Social and economic driving forces	stable and development-stimulating economic policy of the state	volatile and nervous economic policy; wobbly, casual and unstable regulatory rules; changes that are sometimes internally contradictory	chaotic, ad hoc and restrictive economic policy; constant state interference in the functioning of the market and entities market; economic policy forces changes in the current behavior of market entities; significant disruptions in trade and monetary relations; recession and inflation
Product	relatively stable business profile and/or production structure; minimal modification of activities and products	gradual changes in the production structure; modernizing products by adding new functional features	high and random frequency of changes in the business profile and/or structure production; a short product life cycle; the surprising appearance of new products
Staff	regulated relations between management and staff	conflicting interests of management and staff; renegotiating contracts collective with unchanged attitudes and behavioral patterns	changes in attitudes and behavior patterns, as well as social preferences; conflicts between management and staff; the possibility of strikes; negotiating new working conditions

Source: Based on Wach (1998), Marchesnay (1994), Olszewska (2008), and Gościński (1989).

Table 2.3   Selected Definitions of Turbulence

Source	Definition
Ansoff (1985)	The turbulence of the company's environment is constantly increasing and there are four main trends defining it: • an increase in the newness of the change – it means that important events in the company are increasingly different from the experience of employees • increase in the intensity of the environment – this means that recognizing and maintaining the relationship between the enterprise and its partners requires intensifying the involvement of resources and attention of the management • an increase in the speed of changes in the environment – means that changes are quick and occur frequently, which means that the company must constantly adapt to changing conditions • increasing complexity of the environment – means that events are becoming less and less predictable
Haffer (2021)	It maintains Ansoff's definition of environmental turbulence, emphasizing the importance of each trend he identified
Perechuda and Sowińska (2008)	A turbulent environment (sometimes called turbulent) requires some anticipation of how the organization will respond, and its participants must take action based on a rapid cycle of knowledge creation or by creating new knowledge
Kotler and Caslione (2009)	The current environment is characterized by fluctuations and rapid changes that cannot be predicted, which increase risk and uncertainty in the operation of every organization
Sull (2009)	Turbulence is a measure of the frequency of unpredictable changes that affect companies' ability to create and maintain value
Janasz et al. (2010)	The modern environment is turbulent (turbulent), because it is characterized by: • complexity – the number of its elements and the relationships between them increase • the speed of changes related to the introduction of more product innovations • process or organizational • intensity, as the company becomes more and more dependent on its environment

(Continued)

Table 2.3 (*Continued*)   Selected Definitions of Turbulence

Source	Definition
	• difficulties in predicting the states and determinants of the environment • high degree of risk of ongoing processes
Masłyk-Musiał et al. (2012)	A turbulent environment is characterized by the fact that changes are frequent, turbulent, and nonlinear, and therefore their course is difficult to predict. Changes in turbulent environments increasingly have the characteristics of chaotic systems, which means that both the nature of the changes and their effects are difficult to predict
Krupski (2011)	The type of environment is related to the responsiveness and predictability of changes in the business environment. There is a strict relationship: the more turbulent the environment of companies, the more of these companies have a resource orientation in strategic management
Rupik (2011)	A desirable feature of enterprise operations in a turbulent environment is to shorten the response time to changes and increase flexibility

Source: Based on Staniec (2017).

(Matejun and Nowicki, 2013). Therefore, it is possible to isolate certain determinants of turbulence, or at least sets of conditions favorable to it, referring to the distinguished characteristics of the environment, not the immediate one, but the distant one, the so-called macro-environment, and the characteristics of individual industries.

The macro-environment, also referred to as the general environment or further environment of the enterprise, is all the conditions in which the enterprise operates and the change of which is impossible or very difficult for the enterprise (due to the amount and scope of resources that would have to be used); therefore, these are the conditions to which the company must adapt (Gierszewska and Romanowska, 2014). The macroenvironment is considered in the following categories:

■ economic environment determined by the condition of the national, regional, and global economies,
■ demographic environment resulting from changes in the population of a given society,

- legal environment resulting from legal provisions,
- international environment resulting from international conditions,
- social environment resulting from the prevailing fashion, lifestyle, or customs and culture prevailing in a given area,
- technological environment, resulting from the level of technical and technological development.

Studying the macroenvironment requires the use of appropriate methods, which include:

- extrapolation of trends,
- strategic gap analysis,
- scenario method,
- Delphi method,

i.e., approximate, narrative methods; the less precise, the more dynamic the environment. By examining the macro-environment, enterprises are able to assess (or at least estimate) the changes taking place there, their nature, and their dynamics. Nowadays, it is believed that the key characteristic of changes in the environment is non-linearity, which, along with the increasing dynamics of change, gives the macro-environment the characteristics of chaos, where even seemingly insignificant causes (at the input) can cause large changes (at the output) (Andersen and Bettis, 2015). The positive feedback loops characteristic of chaos, in turn, result in increasing marginal revenues (Arthur, 1996) and, as a result, the development of companies that can take advantage of opportunities emerging in a volatile, chaotic environment. An opportunity is defined as a circumstance favorable to something, making something possible, a situation suitable for something, a favorable moment, or an opportunity (Mary George et al., 2016). An opportunity is a combination of circumstances, time, and place that, when combined with some action on the part of the organization, can produce benefits (Sharplin, 1985). Next to the opportunity category, there is the opportunity category as a favorable opportunity (Trzcieliński, 2011). In the business context, opportunities are situations in which new goods, services, materials, or organizational methods can be sold at a price higher than the price of their production (Shane and Venkataraman, 2000), Although such an interpretation is quite narrow and limited to an economic approach, it does not emphasize the rarity and transience of the event or circumstances, which seem to be inherent features of the occasion (Lumpkin et al., 2004). However, it points to the issue of introducing innovations, so it refers to the second of the mentioned areas determining turbulence, namely the industry. In the economy, some industries are highly susceptible to the introduction of new organizational and technical solutions (IT, telecommunications), these are assumed to operate in more turbulent conditions (due to the greater dynamics of changes and emerging opportunities), there are also stable industries, in which changes are initiated rarely and implemented gradually (machinery construction industry).

In the modern economy, adaptation to the macro-environment consists in the ability to use opportunities occurring in the form of events or combinations of various circumstances, of an economic nature (or with economic effects), creating the possibility of achieving additional benefits, material and/or intangible values, related to the moment of time and duration. It is therefore important to identify an opportunity and act on it in a way that allows you to achieve benefits in the form of a competitive advantage.

The source of turbulence is therefore the macro-environment as such, and the phenomena occurring in it, such as globalization and the resulting increasing intensity of competition, which translate into the need to develop and implement innovations in science and technology (Mary George et al., 2016), influence the scope and intensity of this phenomenon.

The relationships between variability, opportunities, competitiveness, and innovation are complex and positive, and the presented phenomena are reinforcing. The variability of the macroenvironment is a source of opportunities; the more opportunities, the greater the variability of the environment. Taking advantage of opportunities contributes to increasing the competitiveness of the company, while the growing intensity of the competitive struggle, in turn, is a source of change and thus turbulence. Volatility causes the need for innovation; the use of opportunities emerging in the environment increases innovation, and thus the variability, strength, and scope of turbulence. The increased level of innovation translates into competitiveness, indirectly strengthening its impact on generating turbulence, and competitiveness strengthens the ability to seize opportunities, which affects innovation. Overlapping dependencies and interactions make the contemporary environment characterized by high intensity and turbulent variability, i.e., turbulence.

The growing turbulence of the environment makes it necessary to change the canons of management from traditional planning, hierarchy, and control to navigation, self-organization, current and strategic adaptability, and also unforced creation. In strategic management, the uncertain environmental context forces flexible approaches to strategy focused on taking advantage of opportunities.

It is therefore not surprising that the scope and scale of turbulent phenomena in a variable and unpredictable environment is the subject of quite widespread interest among management specialists, and the question about the scope and scale of the occurrence of the turbulent environment of enterprises, and therefore the scope and scale of the need to apply new management, is an issue addressed in scientific publications (Krupski, 2013).

Enterprises striving to adapt to the market, and therefore to changes occurring in it, must learn to identify them, accept their consequences and adapt to them, which in turn is all the more difficult the more dynamic and unpredictable the change is (Rokita, 2009). The pace of change is a key category determining the adaptability of an enterprise. The greater the pace of changes in the environment, the greater the (forced) pace of changes in the organization, and the greater the risk for the enterprise related to exposure and even loss of continuity and stability of its functioning. An enterprise, as an open and dynamic system, is characterized by flexibility and adaptability, which, however, are limited primarily by the stability of the system and the ability to maintain a state of balance and homeostasis. Therefore, there are certain limits to the organization's adaptation to external changes and limits to its internal adaptability (Mary George et al., 2016). Within these boundaries, the company can react in two ways to the increasing turbulence and, consequently, the unpredictability of the environment (Lumpkin et al., 2004). Hence, the change is a disruption that can be responded to through proper preparation, the implementation of appropriate structures and processes, and their improvement in response to deviations from the assumed state of the environment. The reactive approach is the result of the adopted approach to changes, based on treating changes as disruptions that can be predicted, so you can also prepare for them, and if this has not been possible so far, it is only due to the imperfection of the forecasting system or the lack of scenarios and models operating in given conditions. The consequence of this assumption is the desire to define and design models for each potential set of conditions, which in turn leads to excessive structuring of activities (Lumpkin et al., 2004). The second model of the company's response is completely different because it assumes that the variability of the environment has the characteristics of chaos and, as such, is not subject to prediction; hence, the company cannot develop appropriate responses; it can only build the potential for variability within the existing strategies, structures, resources, and processes, ensuring flexibility and even leading to chaos (assumed to be controlled) in the organization (Mary George et al., 2016).

The turbulence metaparadigm therefore influences the approach, methods, and techniques used to a significant extent, for example, by the fact that the increase in environmental turbulence limits the effectiveness of forecasts; the greater the intensity of this turbulence, the longer the planning horizon (Krupski, 2011). Therefore, a natural consequence of adopting this paradigm would be the rejection of forecasts as a tool of low effectiveness and, as a result, the abandonment of planning, especially long-term planning, due to the low degree of credibility of plans on such a horizon. However, according to R. Krupski's approach, giving up planning due to the low effectiveness of forecasts would be not only methodologically incorrect but also ontologically incorrect. Krupski postulates that to change the approach to strategy goals, because traditional long-term goals significantly limit the company's flexibility, strategic goals should be formulated in a more flexible and therefore general way, or the strategy should be based on the principles of operation of the organization, setting a filter framework for opportunities arising in the environment or in the organization itself. Building the above-mentioned variability potential requires the use of best practices in the processes implemented by the enterprise, not only key ones, but also auxiliary or supporting ones, and the implementation of active (Pierścionek, 2003) competitive strategies. It can therefore be concluded that the consequence of environmental turbulence is the achievement of a whole range of effects desired by the enterprise, such as flexibility, creativity and management innovation.

The concept of turbulence in the environment is associated with dynamics, without indicating whether the dynamics are caused by a change in the pattern of the environment or in the preferences, actions, or nature of the parties involved. Others treat turbulence as a multidimensional construct that includes environmental elements and define it in the context of market growth. Turbulence in the environment makes it challenging, that is, difficult to survive in, as companies must adapt to:

■ relatively unpredictable changes in the environment (high dynamics),
■ competitive markets, with critical and scarce resources (hostility, competitiveness),

- close links between companies and their suppliers, distributors, customers, and competitors (high complexity),
- diversified products, customers, and businesses (high differentiation).

The adaptation results in endogenous changes, as presented in further chapters.

2.1.2 Sustainability in an Organization's Environment

Sustainability seems to be the opposite of turbulence, as it suggests balance. Sustainable development is a doctrine of political economy having its source in the concepts of natural resource management, according to which further development of humanity is possible if the management of available resources is sustainable. The concept of sustainable management has developed in an evolutionary manner, gaining in scale and importance, starting with the so-called The Brundtland Report, which was prepared by the World Commission on Environment and Development. The document was published in 1987 under the title "Our Common Future", referring to the development of civilization as a whole and pointing to the common responsibility of all countries in this respect. As a result of the analysis of the current social (including demographic), economic, and ecological situation, the authors of the report came to the conclusion that the only way to ensure a safe (in the context of the availability of natural resources and quality of life) future and development for subsequent generations is a global approach to the economy, developing it and managing it in a sustainable way (Williams et al., 2017).

Balancing is about taking into account environmental issues, by striving to implement economic processes in such a way that they contribute to solving ecological problems both on a local and global scale (or at least do not lead to their escalation), social, through fair functioning on the market, in attitude towards the law, competition, and own employees (implementation of the concept of fair trade, Corporate Social Responsibility), and economic, by striving to maximize the company's value and meet the needs and expectations of customers (Lindgreen and Swaen, 2010). Sustainable management therefore appears as the opposite of an exploitative economy, focused on selected aspects or industries, and based on the iron rule of Malthus's economics, pointing to the need for a comprehensive (holistic) approach to management, treating the global economic system as linked by the material,

financial, and social relations systems of individual countries. Such an interpretation not only shows but even highlights the inequalities and hetero-
geneity of the system, while at the same time providing the opportunity,
through the identified connections, to balance the existing dispropor-
tions. Additionally, it also draws attention to the limited nature of available
resources and the particular importance of managing them sustainably so as
to ensure the availability and security of resources for as long as possible,
enabling future generations to meet their needs. Referring to the document
base for the concept of sustainable development, the above-mentioned
Brundtland Report, it should be emphasized that, resulting from the diagnosis and forecast presented therein regarding the future state of the economy,
there is a need to promote and implement sustainable development, which
is defined as development that meets the needs of the present without limiting future opportunities for generations to meet their own needs. Within this
definition, two key concepts can be identified:

■ the concept of "needs", especially the basic needs of poor people and
societies, which should be treated as a clear priority,
■ the concept of limitations resulting from the level of technology and
organization of societies and the ability of the natural environment to
meet these needs.

Therefore, the essence of sustainable development is a process of change
in which the exploitation of resources, the direction of investments, the
orientation of technological development, and institutional changes are
harmonized to enable the fulfillment of human needs and aspirations, both
now and in the future. The current level of prosperity can be maintained if
managed properly. The model of such an economy assumes appropriately
and consciously shaped relationships between economic growth, care for
the environment (not only natural but also artificial and man-made), and
the quality of life (including human health). The doctrine of sustainable
development strives for social justice through, among others, the economic
and environmental effectiveness of projects ensured, among others, by a
strict calculation of production costs, which also extends in a very complex
way to external resources (Stanton, 2012). The theory of public good is also
widely used in the economics of sustainable development (Tietenberg and
Lewis, 2008), and the most frequently indicated goal of sustainable development is the increase of social and individual well-being and the harmonious

arrangement of relations between man and nature, the satisfaction of basic needs necessary for proper physical and mental health of a human being, i.e., achieving the so-called balanced quality of life (Zaufal, 1987). However, sustainable development is not only about social issues. In economics, it is assumed that it is a theory that comprehensively addresses the problem of the long-term ability of the modern economy to develop while meeting the criterion of intergenerational justice, which "consists in maximizing the net benefits from economic development while protecting and ensuring the reproduction of the usefulness and quality of natural resources over a long period of time. Economic development must then mean not only an increase in per capita income, but also an improvement in other elements of social well-being. It must also include the necessary structural changes in the economy and in society as a whole" (Turner & Pearce, 1990). In turn, from the point of view of the natural environment, sustainable development was defined, among others, in the World Conservation Strategy developed by the International Union for Conservation of Nature (IUCN) in cooperation with the United Nations Environment Program (UNEP) and the World Wide Fund for Nature (WWF) in the 1980s. The strategy, signed by the Secretary-General of the United Nations and published simultaneously in 34 capitals of the world, has become the basis for a comprehensive view of environmental protection and the sustainable use of natural resources, defining sustainable development as (UNEP) "the transformation of the biosphere and the use of human, economic, and inanimate nature resources and revitalized to meet people's needs and improve the quality of their lives, which takes into account social, ecological, and economic factors, the amount of natural resources, and, in the case of choosing one of the development options, the benefits and losses resulting from this choice". The use of economic, ecological, and social perspectives has resulted in the development of many definitions of sustainable development; their multitude and diversity are reflected in numerous models of implementation and implementation of the concept of sustainable development in the economy and result in an evolutionary expansion of the scale and meaning of the concept itself. Key achievements in this area and their nature are presented in Table 2.4.

Table 2.4 shows the transition from identifying resource-related problems (related to the limited nature of natural resources) to attempts and proposals for their solutions, both on a global scale and in individual business units. It is also possible to notice how ad hoc solutions, often of

Table 2.4   Milestones in Sustainability Concept Development

Changes, Events, and Achievements in the Concept of Sustainable Development	Domain
Including environmental protection issues in the scope of state functions and tasks (*The Declaration of the United Nations Conference on the Human Environment*)	Politics
Use of the term sustainable development in the global Nature Conservation Strategy (World Conservation Strategy, Living Resource Conservation for Sustainable Development, IUCN, UNEP, WWF 1980)	Ecology
Development of the so-called The Brundtland Report and the definition of sustainable development (*Our Common Future*)	Macroeconomy,
Popularization of the concept of sustainable development at the Earth Summit in Rio de Janeiro (*United Nations Conference on Environment and Development*, UNCED)	Macroeconomy, politics
Introduction of the *triple bottom line* (corporate sustainability) (Elkington, 1997)	Business
Linking the management of natural resources with the management of enterprise resources (Hart, 1995)	Business
Development of a model of interconnections between the enterprise and the ecosystem (Jennings and Zandbergen, 1995)	Business, science
Identification of relationships between the environment, resource efficiency, level of innovation, and competitiveness (Porter and van der Linde, 1997).	Macroeconomy, business, science
Incorporating sustainable development into corporate strategies. Identification of the importance of applied technologies for sustainable development (Hart, 1997)	Business, ecology
A management approach based on the use of environmental opportunities (Reinhardt, 1999)	Business, ecology
Changes in business practices include increasing the efficiency of natural resources, moving to biologically inspired production systems, process-based business models, and investing in natural capital (Lovins et al., 1999)	Business, ecology, science

(Continued)

Table 2.4 (*Continued*)   Milestones in Sustainability Concept Development

Changes, Events, and Achievements in the Concept of Sustainable Development	Domain
A three-part strategy using the achievements of various sciences to increase economic and environmental efficiency, interpreting sustainable development through the prism of added value for stakeholders (Holliday, 2001)	Business, science
World Summit on Sustainable Development in Johannesburg	Macroeconomy
Interpreting sustainable development as a goal or task (Graedel and Klee, 2002)	Macroeconomy, business
The increasing importance of sustainable development for creating value for stakeholders (Hart and Milstein, 2003)	Business
Identification of properties of sustainable systems (Fiksel, 2003)	Science
Embedding sustainable development in science as a certain scientific sub- or meta-discipline (Mihlecic et al., 2003)	Science
Development of models, tools, and theories supporting the implementation of the concept of sustainable development (Anastas and Zimerman, 2003; Hardjono and Klein, 2004)	Science
Systems research in the context of social, economic, and ecological factors (Cabezas et al., 2003, 2005, 2007)	Science, macroeconomy
Developing a hierarchy within sustainable development (referring to Maslow's pyramid of needs) (Marshall and Toffel, 2005)	Science
Developing models for enterprises striving for sustainable development (Dunphy et al., 2003; Young and Tilley, 2006; Dyllick and Hockerts, 2002; McDonough and Braungart, 2002; Gladwin et al., 1995)	Science
Developing principles of sustainable business conduct at the operational level (Unruh, 2008)	Science, business
Development of the Europe 2020 strategy	Macroeconomy

Source: Own work based on Wysokińska-Senkus (2013).

the nature of best practices, gained a scientific dimension through generalization, the development of model solutions, and research. The works, projects, and research mentioned refer both to general characteristics and the strategic aspect of sustainable development, as well as to issues of an operational implementation nature. They pay attention to aspects of resource consumption, integrating ecological and economic issues. Hence, the exogenous concept of sustainability leads to the topic of resources, representing endogenous aspects of management.

2.2   Endogenous Approach to Changes

The issue of enterprise resources is inextricably linked to management theory and economics and has already appeared in the thought of classical economists (Kunasz, 2006). Resources originally defined as production factors were referred to by, among others: W. Petty, A. Smith, D. Ricardo, J. B. Say, K. Marks, A. Marshall, J. B.Clark, J. Mill, and J. R. MacCulloch, pointing out the importance of work, qualifications, tools, and capital for the economy as a whole and for individual economic processes.

Schumpeter considered innovations introduced by entrepreneurs to be crucial to achieving profit and economic development and growth. He understood innovations as new combinations of material elements and human productive power, the essence of which is to produce a new product or introduce a product with new properties to the market, use a new production method, find a new sales market, acquire new sources of raw materials, or introduce a new production organization (Schumpeter, 1960). The ability to undertake innovative activities results in achieving a competitive advantage (Sulimowska-Formowicz, 2002). E. Penrose, in turn, emphasized that an enterprise is a unique set of production resources that can be used in various ways, this diversity translates into uniqueness and, consequently, the ability to gain a competitive advantage (Penrose, 1959). The beginnings of the resource-based trend in science date back to the 1950s, and the evolution in identifying sources of competitive advantage during this period is presented in Table 2.5.

The exogenous perspective was presented as a starting point, in which the acquisition of new markets and the development of new products were of key importance; markets and products were seen as opportunities, therefore they were treated as starting points for development goals and sources of competitive advantage (innovation according to Schumpeter).

Table 2.5 Exogenous and Endogenous Goals

	Exogenous Perspective	The Classical Endogenous Perspective	Endogenous Non-Classical Perspective
Categories of description of development goals	Products, markets	Products, markets	Resources, competences
Starting points for generating development goals	Products, markets as opportunities	Resources, competences as strong points	Resources, competences as strong points dedicated to benefit from opportunities

Source: Krupski (2010).

The exogenous perspective used the analysis of competitive forces developed by Porter (Porter and van der Linde, 1995; Kunasz, 2006) to identify ways to exploit opportunities emerging in the environment. The change from the exogenous to the endogenous perspective was the result of the growing influence of the resource-based approach on management sciences. The resource approach again indicated that the phenomenon of endogenous growth was already present in the works of A. Smith (Kunasz, 2006), shifted the emphasis to the inside of the company, and restored interest in resources. The endogenous approach has been developing particularly dynamically since the 1990s, when the work of J. Barney was published (Szymaniec, 2012), referring to the so-called resource approach – RBV (Resource-Based View of the Firm). A milestone in its development was the research of J. Barney, but also of B. Wernerfelt (1984) and R. P. Rumelt (1991). The resource-based theory presents an enterprise as a unique bundle of tangible and intangible resources and skills that, thanks to their characteristics, constitute a source of sustainable competitive advantage (Barney, 1991; Amit and Schoemaker, 1993).

In this approach, achieving a sustainable competitive advantage results from having resources of strategic value. However, the relationship between resources, strategic value, and sustainable competitive advantage is simplified and is based on the assumption that good company performance is synonymous with gaining a competitive advantage (Barney, 1991). However, the analysis of the relationship between resources and the company's results leads to the conclusion that the relationship between these values is not causal, and the company's results are only a derivative of the competitive advantage obtained thanks to strategic activities implemented using strategic resources. The determinants of a company's success refer to having so-called strategic resources, or resources of strategic value. Traditional management concepts sought competitive advantage and strategic value in material resources, such as raw materials, capital or location (Sajdak, 2010). Nowadays, both in the classical and non-classical endogenous approaches, greater value is assigned to intangible resources and competences, because they, due to their properties, allow for achieving a competitive advantage. Competitive advantage resulting from the use of key competencies (including extraordinary skills, knowledge, and the reputation of the company) may be the basis for strategic competitiveness. Therefore, the key development goal is not the development of markets but the development of competences, which is expressed in the non-classical endogenous approach – the last stage in the evolution of the enterprise's development goals so far. Competencies are treated as the company's strengths, thanks to which it is possible to take advantage of emerging opportunities in the environment and thus strengthen its competitive position. The role of resources in gaining a competitive advantage is therefore crucial, and the development of resources, primarily intangible ones, in the form of competences, is the basic development goal of enterprises.

2.2.1 Definition and Classification of Resources

Due to its importance for competitiveness, a resource is one of the key categories in economics. It is a certain amount of something that has been collected or accumulated for future use; it is something that exists, a reserve, an economic quantity, the state of which is measured at a specific moment (it has no time dimension) (Stachowiak and Stachowiak, 2015); and are things used to produce goods and services. Resources, according to the APICS (American Production and Inventory Control Society) dictionary, are everything that is needed to produce a product, and the lack of which would result in failure to implement the adopted production plan. In this sense, resources are raw materials and materials (both basic and auxiliary), potential measured by the time of availability of machines and employees with appropriate competences, power supplies, and money (APICS) (Table 2.6).

Table 2.6 Selected Definitions of Resources

Author/s	Definition
Wernerfelt (1984)	Resources represent what can be perceived as a strength or weakness of an enterprise
Barney (1991)	Resources include all assets, organizational processes, company attributes, information, knowledge, etc. under the company's control and enabling the design and implementation of a strategy that increases efficiency.
Grant (1991)	Resources are inputs in the process of creating value by an enterprise
Amit and Schoemaker (1993)	Resources include the set of assets owned or controlled by an enterprise
Teece et al. (1997)	Resources are assets specific to a given company that are difficult or even impossible to copy by competitors

Source: Matwiejczuk (2014).

Key resource characteristics desirable for their potential to create a competitive advantage include:

- value,
- rarity,
- difficulty of imitation and substitution (Barney, 1991).

From a different perspective, the following features are important:

- scarcity,
- low mobility,
- limited imitability,
- substitutability,
- possibility of appropriation,
- durability,
- mutual complementation,
- alignment with strategic industry factors (Amit, 1993).

There is also another formulation of the factors determining the value of resources in the literature, namely:

- imperfect imitation,
- imperfect substitutability,
- imperfect mobility,
- diversity,
- limitations (Peteraf, 1993);

or also:

- imperfect imitation,
- durability,
- possibility of appropriation,
- substitutability,
- excellence (Collins and Montgomery, 1995).

The presented characteristics present a basically consistent view, emphasizing the impact of the difficulty of imitation on the importance of resources. The difficulty of imitation reflects the degree of impossibility of copying a given resource due to its physical uniqueness, the need for accumulation over time, a specific development path, unprofitability, and the ambiguity of cause and effect relationships occurring within a given bundle of assets (Dytwald, 1996). Another recurring feature is substitutability, i.e. the limited possibility of replacing a given resource with another one representing the same or very similar properties.

In an integrated approach, the desired resources that enable achieving sustainable competitive advantage and organizational success are those that meet the so-called the VRIN condition, i.e. characterized by strategic value (V-Valuable), rarity (R-Rare), non-imitability (I-Inimitable) and having no substitutes (N-Non-substitutable) (Barney, 1991), rarity, low mobility, limited imitability, substitutability, appropriability, durability, mutual complementation, fit to strategic industry factors (Amit and Schoemaker, 1993) and imperfect imitability, imperfect substitutability, imperfect mobility, diversity, ex ante and ex post constraints (Peteraf, 1993), the concepts of other authors extended and integrated the presented lists (Dytwald, 1996). This configuration of resources should constitute the basis for formulating a strategy.

From the point of view of resource management, in addition to their characteristics, the classification of resources is also important, so that management methods and tools can be appropriately selected for the distinguished groups of resources with common characteristics. Examples of resource classifications presented in the literature are listed in Table 2.7.

One of the most frequently proposed ways of classifying resources is the division into tangible and intangible, but this is not the only approach to classifying resources used in the context of management science or practice.

Some authors, in addition to tangible and intangible resources, mention organizational and information resources (Barney, 1991). However, while tangible components of resources, i.e. material, human, and financial resources,

Table 2.7 Resources Classification

Authors	Criterion	Resources
Say (2001)	Type	Land – the primary factor of production Work – people with their qualifications, skills, experience and abilities Capital – all the physical elements of a property
Grant (1991)	Competitive Edge creation	Financial resources Physical resources Human resources Technology resources Image and reputation resources Organizational resources
Barney (1991)	Competitive Edge importance	Financial capital – is perceived as an essential resource from the point of view of strategy and includes not only the money and other assets owned by the company, but also the possibility of obtaining financial resources from external sources and future profits Physical capital – it consists of all tangible assets and technologies used resulting from the machines and devices owned and the IT systems used Human capital – means the skills, experience, intellectual potential and personality traits of individual employees Organizational capital – covers many elements of the organization, including: organizational structure, organizational culture, management methods, relations within the enterprise, relations with the environment

(Continued)

Table 2.7 (*Continued*)   Resources Classification

Authors	Criterion	Resources
Klasik (1993)	Strategy	Human resources – these include, among others: qualifications and preparation of human resources, skills and competences, quality of management, organizational culture, Technical resources – these include, among others: production capacity, modern equipment, research potential, Commercial resources – these include the quality and variety of goods and services, the brand and the distribution network Financial resources – include, among others: cash flow, self-financing ability, debt level
Black and Boal (1992)	Interpretation range	Partial resources System resources
Collins and Montgomery (1995)	Nature of resources	Material resources Intangible resources Abilities
Miller and Shamsie (1965)	Source of resources	Ownership-based resources Knowledge-based resources
Durand (1997)	Nature of resources	Knowledge resources (explicit and tacit) Abilities Brands and trade names
Sanchez and Heene (1996)	Source of resources	Resources owned Resources that can be obtained by the enterprise
Fahy and Smithee (1999)	Nature of resources	Material resources Intangible resources Abilities
Bratnicki (1999)	Competitive Edge perspective	Material resources Financial resources Market resources – refer to the product brand, customer loyalty, reputation, distribution channels Intellectual property – patents, copyrights, industrial designs, know-how, databases

(Continued)

Table 2.7 (*Continued*)   **Resources Classification**

Authors	Criterion	Resources
		Human resources – knowledge, experience, judgment, intelligence, skills Organizational processes – management systems, organizational structure, organizational processes and procedures Relational resources – the entire set of ties of a given enterprise that enable it to influence economic reality
Hafeez et al. (2002)	Nature of resources	Physical resources Intellectual resources Cultural resources
Sanchez and Heene (2004)	Value creation perspective	Assets include everything that the organization uses to achieve its goals and contributes to creating value in the enterprise (directly or indirectly), assets may be tangible and intangible Skills – defined as repetitive patterns of activities (related to the use of assets) in the enterprise, belong to the resources related to the operation Knowledge – defined as the basis of every activity in the enterprise, the key task of strategic managers is to identify and acquire many different sources of knowledge necessary to maintain and develop the value creation process in the organization
Rokita (2005)	Competitive Edge perspective	People – staff and qualifications Physical – factories, equipment, inventory Financial – receivables, capital, liquidity Perceptual – customers, suppliers, competitors Political – the government and its agencies Organizational – culture, system, structure, decision-making processes Knowledge – evolution of the sector, macroeconomic changes, technologies

(Continued)

Table 2.7 (*Continued*)   Resources Classification

Authors	Criterion	Resources
de Wit and Mayer (2007)	Importance of resources	Material resources – these include the so-called visible resources, e.g. land, machines, buildings, equipment, money (cash, highly liquid assets) Intangible resources – these include the so-called invisible resources, e.g. relational resources, such as relationships with suppliers, customers, the environment, reputation, brand awareness and skills which include knowledge, innovative capabilities in terms of products and processes, integration capabilities
Obłój (2007)	Origin of resources	Source resources – are a derivative of natural conditions or include experience accumulated during the existence of the organization, including all resources at the disposal of the enterprise Operational resources – related to the method of use, use and creation of source resources Situational resources – their occurrence is difficult to predict because they result from opportunities occurring within the enterprise and its ongoing

Source: Based on Matwiejczuk (2014).

can be valued and quantitatively examined, intangible resources are difficult to objectively value (Kunasz, 2006); however, due to their characteristics, including those relating to the VRIN criterion, intangible resources are now perceived as key to a company's competitiveness. A hierarchy of resources reflecting this view is proposed by Rybak (2003). At the lowest level of the hierarchy, ordered according to increasing value and difficulty of imitation, resources in the strict sense (material resources) are located; the following levels include abilities, competencies, and key competencies.

It is debatable to clearly define the category of intangible resources; hence, further fragmentation is considered advisable. Generally, we distinguish capabilities, competencies, and key competencies, but the fragmentation of intangible resources may be more far-reaching. The approaches proposed in this regard are presented in Table 2.8 and include (Hall, 1992):

Table 2.8 Intangible Resources

	Functional	Cultural	Positional	Regulative	
Dependent on humans	Knowledge and skills of employees, suppliers and distributors	Organizational culture, ability to learn			Skills
			Reputation, networks		Resources
Independent on humans			Databases, information	Contracts, licenses, trade secrets, property rights	

Source: Hall (1992).

- assets and skills,
- resources dependent and independent of people,
- protected and unprotected resources.

To sum up, resources are a broad and heterogeneous category, which results in difficulties in proposing coherent models and approaches to their management.

2.2.1.1 Industry 4.0

Contemporary approaches to resources are often based on the concept of Industry 4.0. The term Industry 4.0 was first used and introduced in Germany during the Hannover Fair in 2011, as a solution to support the competitiveness of German industry. The definition of the term is quite vague and usually involves reference to the evolution of the economy and industry (Toeffler, 1995):

1. The first wave was agrarian, which was related, according to Toffler, to the appearance of inventions and skills related to agriculture and the popularization of a sedentary lifestyle about 10,000 years ago;
2. The second wave is industrial, the emergence of industrialism associated with the invention of printing and the steam engine; a wave rising about 300 years ago brought steel production, electricity, new means of

transport and mass communication, standardization, and uniformity; the second wave is usually connected with the first and second industrial revolutions, changes in industry involving steam power implementation, mechanization of manufacturing processes, and consequent mass production with the use of assembly lines;

3. The third wave, currently experienced, is directly related to the emergence of new technologies enabling unlimited communication between individuals thanks to the development of services and the departure from mass production; the third wave covers the third and fourth industrial revolutions, namely automation and its consequences, followed by advanced digital technology development.

The Fourth Industrial Revolution is also referred to as Industry 4.0 and is presented in the context of advanced technologies, including AI, IoT, robotics, 3D printing, and others. The important thing is that Industry 4.0 is not a set of advanced solutions; it is focused on the integration of intelligent machines and solutions. If they cooperate and share the resources, the industry is at the 4.0 level, and the economy is perceived as Economy 4.0, benefiting from contemporary solutions (Ávila-Gutiérrez et al., 2019). Economy 4.0 is a term used to describe the social, political, and business-related conditions resulting from the implementation of Fourth Industrial Revolution (Industry 4.0) technologies and trends. It refers to the economic consequences of the integration of advanced digital technologies, automation, connectivity, and data-driven decision-making, as these solutions are transforming how goods and services are produced, distributed, and consumed. Economy 4.0 is characterized by increased productivity, efficiency, and innovation resulting from changes in information flows, including digital transformation and implementation of artificial intelligence, cloud computing, and big data analytics into decision-making processes, as well as changes in material flows resulting from automation of production processes, the implementation of robotics, and autonomous manufacturing and logistics processes. These solutions lead to a shift (Greiff and Kyllonen, 2016) in the capacity size and profile required, as direct labor and its cost are decreased, while demand for advanced skills is growing as digital, automated, and autonomous solutions need to be designed, programmed, and maintained. The transition to Economy 4.0 requires a skilled workforce capable of adapting to rapidly changing information and manufacturing technologies. Other consequences of advanced solution implementation are product- and service- oriented. Implementation of advanced solutions for manufacturing and logistics can decrease the number of errors caused by humans, and together with improved quality control processes, also equipped with contemporary technologies, can increase the quality of products and services. Economy 4.0 is changing companies and markets as it naturally benefits from connectivity and ICT to boost business activity (Gobble, 2018). Implementation of digital platforms and e-commerce solutions changes local supply chains and networks into global structures interconnected and integrated on many levels, exploiting new business opportunities. New opportunities are often followed by new challenges and the need to adjust the business model to the needs and constraints of contemporary global markets. Emerging business models are more flexible, asset-light, sharing economy, and circular economy oriented, e.g., subscription services, PaaS (Product as a Service), and platform-based services. These days finding customers and reaching them is fast and easy thanks to real-time communication and access to the Internet, whereas maintaining customers and gaining their loyalty is difficult as there are many opportunities available and customers benefit from world-wide access to products and services. Information on market offer is used by customers and enables them to select the best-fit products and services, but it is also available for businesses. Demand size and profile, expectations, and requirements recognition are crucial for forecasting and developing customized and personalized offers. Together with data retrieved from manufacturing processes, machine performance, and process parameters, it creates a dataset that enables informed decision-making and optimization of operations. As the datasets are huge (sometimes the big data term is rephrased to gigantic data), advanced analytics and machine learning need to be implemented to benefit from the information potential created thanks to digital transformation and Economy 4.0 (Chen et al., 2016).

Overall, Economy 4.0 represents a paradigm shift in management, emphasizing digital innovation, agility, and resilience in the face of technological disruption and global challenges. It offers opportunities for businesses to grow, improve their competitiveness, and operate in a sustainable and responsible way. Thanks to access to multiple data sources, it provides a holistic understanding of business, embracing economic aspects together with environmental issues and societal challenges of aging societies and the requirements of digital literacy, technical skills, and lifelong learning that are essential to ensure workforce readiness and competitiveness in the digital economy.

However, to make Economy 4.0 and Industry 4.0 work integration of multiple solutions is essential.

Integration of intelligent machines and solutions requires technological and organizational transformation of companies (Shaw et al., 1992); hence, Industry 4.0 is a driver for endogenous changes.

The goal of the industrial revolution is increased digitization, mobility, and the transformation of value chains.

Digitization (Gobble, 2018) is the process of gradually introducing digital technology into the environment around us. In practice, digitization means transforming information from analog to digital form. Thanks to this, data that was previously stored in paper, audio, or image form is now saved in the form of binary code.

Digitization enables the transfer of traditional paper documents and processes to modern electronic platforms, which allows for the automation of many activities and the improvement of work efficiency and speed.

Modern companies are increasingly choosing to digitize their processes and documents. Thanks to this, they can reduce the time and costs associated with performing business activities, which translates into the company's greater competitiveness on the market.

It is worth noting that digitization differs from digitalization, which involves transforming data in paper form into electronic form. Digitization is a broader process that includes not only digitization but also many other activities related to the implementation and use of digital technologies.

Digitization enabled the introduction and implementation of the Internet of Things (IoT) (Mukhopadhyay and Suryadevara, 2014). The IoT is a network of interconnected devices that can communicate and exchange data with each other over the Internet without the need for human intervention. The interconnected devices in a manufacturing context are machines, processing centers, etc., and the concept/solution is referred to as the IIoT (Industrial Internet of Things). Communication is enabled by sensors, actuators, and software for collecting and exchanging data connected to the Internet or local networks. The efficiency of communication depends on technologies used, which include Wi-Fi, Bluetooth, RFID, and cellular networks. To support data storage, cloud-based platforms are used. Data stored is processed, and in many cases, it needs to be processed in real time. Techniques such as big data analytics, machine learning, and neural networks are employed for extracting and processing data retrieved from sensors so that it can be used for decision-making and action-initiating. Expected benefits include, among others, increased productivity, improved decision-making, and process automation. Implementation of IoT/IIoT brings numerous benefits but also generates risks emerging from the sensitive nature of data collected by devices. Thus, security and privacy should be provided, and the solutions suggested are encryption, authentication, access controls, and regular software updates. These security measures are supposed to protect IoT/IIoT from cyber threats.

The IoT has the potential to revolutionize industries, improve quality of life and drive innovation by enabling seamless connectivity and intelligent automation in various fields. Implementation of IoT/IIoT results in creating connections between devices and initiates the transformation of manufacturing systems into CPS (Cyber-Physical Systems).

A CPS (Alguliyev et al., 2018) is an integration of computational elements and physical components that are deeply interconnected and interact with each other in real time. These systems link the cyberworld of computing and communication with the physical world, where the actions of the physical components are controlled or influenced by the computational elements. These connections result in increased potential for manufacturing systems. Their key characteristics include features that are also characteristics of IoT/IIoT (Sisinni et al., 2018):

- Interconnectivity: CPS components, which can include sensors, actuators, controllers, and computing devices, are interconnected through networks, enabling communication and coordination between them.
- Interaction: CPS components interact with each other and with the physical environment in real time, often requiring rapid and precise responses to changing conditions or events.
- Sensitivity: CPS includes sensors to collect data from the physical environment and actuators to control physical processes or devices based on the collected data.
- Complexity: CPS typically involves embedded systems, where software and hardware are tightly integrated to perform specific tasks efficiently and reliably.
- Responsiveness: Many CPS employ feedback control loops to continuously monitor the system's behavior, compare it to the desired performance or state, and adjust system parameters or actions accordingly.

The CPS concept is universal and not limited to industrial automation. It can be implemented in autonomous vehicles, since cars, drones, and other vehicles equipped with sensors, processors, and actuators are able to perceive the environment and make decisions without human intervention, as well as in smart buildings, which are equipped with interconnected systems for monitoring and controlling heating, ventilation, air conditioning (HVAC), lighting, and security to improve energy efficiency and occupant comfort. In the social context, CPS can be implemented in healthcare systems, medical devices, wearable sensors, and monitoring systems that collect and analyze patient data to provide personalized healthcare services and support remote patient monitoring. Generally, the role of CPS is vital for advancing technology across various sectors by enabling greater automation, efficiency, and integration between the digital and physical worlds.

The integration between the digital and physical world is the result of the combination of different technologies and systems. Its goal is to increase the efficiency of processes, facilitate monitoring and analysis, and accelerate the digital transformation. Hence, integration of intelligent machines and devices is a key aspect of Industry 4.0; connecting different systems and technologies enables cooperation and resource sharing.

The integration is supported by automation (Jämsä-Jounela, 2007). Automation reduces manual operations in many areas. It can be applied across various functions and departments within an organization, including manufacturing and production. Automation technologies such as robotics, programmable logic controllers (PLCs), and computer numerical control (CNC) systems are used to automate manufacturing processes, assembly lines, and industrial tasks. Automation requires investments in infrastructure purchase and integration but it brings substantial benefits. They include improved accuracy, speed, and consistency in production, leading to higher throughput, lower costs, and improved quality control.

Automation can be limited to a single organization; however, in the global supply chain era, it is most likely to be spread across the entire supply chain. Automation in supply chain management (Nitsche et al., 2021) involves the use of software tools and technologies to automate procurement, inventory management, logistics, and distribution processes; hence, it is not limited to the automation of manufacturing processes. Automated systems supporting supply chains enable real-time tracking of goods, optimization of transportation routes, and just-in-time inventory management, reducing lead times and improving supply chain efficiency. Implementation of automation in supply chains requires a wide range of integration, not only of equipment (technical devices) but also of IT systems and management procedures. The multi-level integration results in reaching the goal of supply chain management, which is high customer service levels and low total costs. Customer service level is traditionally expressed in reduced response time, yet the expectations of customers are continuously growing. The trend recognized these days is the need for customized service. Hence, automation supports functions to streamline interactions and enhance the customer experience. Chatbots, virtual assistants, and automated ticketing systems can handle routine inquiries, provide self-service options, and escalate complex issues to human agents, improving efficiency and scalability in customer service operations. Hence, customer service is one of the processes efficiently supported by automation. Others include:

- Finance and accounting (Doguc, 2021): automation is employed in finance and accounting functions to facilitate financial processes, automate repetitive tasks, and improve accuracy in financial reporting and analysis. Automated systems can handle repetitive tasks such as invoice processing, expense management, reconciliation, and financial forecasting, enabling finance teams to focus on creative strategic initiatives and decision-making.
- Human resources (HR) management (Kazakovs et al., 2015): automation in HR involves the use of software platforms and tools to automate recruitment, onboarding, offboarding, payroll processing, performance management, and, to some extent, employee training. Automated HR systems improve efficiency, compliance, and employee engagement by reducing manual administrative tasks and providing self-service capabilities for employees.
- Marketing and Sales (Järvinen and Taiminen, 2016): automation is used in marketing and sales functions to support customer segmentation, and campaign management processes. Automated marketing platforms enable personalized communication, optimize marketing campaigns, improve conversion rates, and increase revenue.
- Data Analysis and Reporting (Sarker, 2023): automation tools and algorithms are used to automate data collection, analysis, and reporting processes, enabling organizations to derive insights from large datasets more efficiently. Automated analytics platforms can perform tasks such as data cleansing, data visualization, predictive modeling, and automated reporting, facilitating data-driven decision-making across the organization.

Automation in companies results in numerous benefits, including improved operational efficiency, cost savings, scalability, accuracy, and agility. However, successful automation implementation requires careful planning, the integration of technologies, change management, and ongoing monitoring and optimization to maximize the value and impact of automation initiatives. The changes are generally focused on technology; however, the implementation of automation results also in organizational changes and new business opportunities. Examples of business models that emerged as a consequence of changes in technology, market conditions, and societal trends and benefit from digital technologies, platforms, and ecosystems disrupting traditional industries include:

■ Subscription-Based Models (Lindström et al., 2023): Companies offer subscription-based services in many industries. The concept is very simple: customers pay a recurring fee for access to products, services, or content. The model is very flexible; customers may resign anytime they want and restart cooperation later. In a post-pandemic, fragile world characterized by uncertainty of income and stability, such an option is very often sought. Examples include streaming platforms, subscription boxes like Birchbox, product-as-a-service (PaaS), and software-as-a-service (SaaS) options.

■ Sharing Economy Platforms (Sutherland and Jarrahi, 2018): They facilitate peer-to-peer transactions, enabling individuals to share resources, assets, and services. Their popularity is a result of a sustainable approach to business and an ecology-oriented society that resells and reuses products. Examples include ride-sharing services, accommodation platforms, and freelancing platforms.

■ Platform-Based Models (Krishnan and Gupta, 2001): Platform-based business models bring together multiple stakeholders, such as buyers, sellers, and service providers, on a digital platform to facilitate transactions, interactions, and value exchange. Examples include e-commerce platforms, gig economy platforms, and social media platforms. The model was impossible before the development of digital technologies and was of limited demand before e-commerce growth, resulting, among others, from pandemic restrictions.

■ Freemium Models (Zennyo, 2020): Companies offer a basic version of their product or service for free, with the option to upgrade to a premium version with additional features or functionality for a fee. This model is consistent with the sustainable approach to the economy, which results in limited resource use and frugal process execution. Examples include freemium mobile apps with in-app purchases, freemium software with premium tiers, and freemium content platforms with subscription options.

- ▪ On-Demand Models (Zardini et al., 2022): On-demand models enable customers to access goods or services immediately, as needed, typically through digital platforms or mobile apps. Examples include food delivery services, transportation services, and home services. Societal changes created the need for fast and customized responses to individual needs and requirements and digital transformation enabled fast and efficient access to information on service options available.
- ▪ Circular Economy Models (Lewandowski, 2016): Circular economy models are a direct consequence of sustainable development principles. They focus on minimizing waste, maximizing resource efficiency, and promoting sustainability by designing products for reuse, recycling, and remanufacturing. Examples include clothing rental services, electronics leasing programs, and product-as-a-service (PaaS) offerings.

And many others, including innovative models, etc.

The list of new business models is dynamically changing and growing. Some of the solutions are widely accepted and have become a regular practice, while others are of limited range and use. New circumstances (business, environmental, and geopolitical) bring new challenges and inspire new approaches and new business models emerge to reshape industries and offer new opportunities for value creation and innovation. As technology continues to evolve and disrupt traditional business models, companies must adapt and innovate to stay competitive in a rapidly changing marketplace. Yet, since most of the new business models exploit digital technologies, what needs to be mentioned is the security aspect. Digital processes and transactions can be compromised, posing significant risks to companies across various industries and impacting their operations, finances, reputation, and customer trust. Parallelly to digital transformation growth and development, cyber threats are becoming more and more serious and dangerous, causing damage in many aspects of companies' performance through data breaches (Kumar et al., 2005). Cyberattacks, such as data breaches, can result in unauthorized access to sensitive information, including customer data, intellectual property, and financial records. Data breaches can lead to financial losses, operations disruptions, regulatory fines, legal liabilities, and damage to brand reputation. They are not only financial losses, even though cybersecurity incidents can cause financial losses due to theft of funds, fraudulent transactions, business disruption, and remediation costs. Companies may incur expenses related to incident response, forensic investigations, data recovery, and legal fees. Operational aspects are also important. Cyberattack may cause serious disruptions to operations. Cyberattacks such as ransomware, distributed denial-of-service (DDoS) attacks, and malware infections can disrupt business operations, leading to downtime, loss of productivity, and disruption of critical services. Operational disruptions can have cascading effects on supply chains, customer service, and revenue generation. Cybersecurity incidents such as system outages, data corruption, and loss of access to IT resources can disrupt critical business functions, including manufacturing, logistics, finance, and customer support. Operational disruptions can lead to delays, service interruptions, and financial losses. Operational problems and financial losses may lead to regulatory compliance issues. Cybersecurity incidents can trigger regulatory compliance issues, particularly in industries subject to data protection and privacy regulations. Companies may face penalties, fines, and legal consequences for non-compliance with data security standards, breach notification requirements, and privacy laws. Cyberattacks are also connected with intellectual property theft. Cyberattacks targeting intellectual property (IP) can result in the theft of trade secrets, proprietary information, and research and development (R&D) data. Intellectual property theft can undermine competitiveness, innovation, and market advantage, leading to a loss of market share and revenue.

The consequence of cyber threats perceived severely is reputational damage which has a long term impact on a company's performance. Cybersecurity breaches can result in reputational damage and the loss of customer trust. Negative publicity, media coverage, and public disclosure of security incidents can erode brand reputation, customer confidence, and stakeholder trust, leading to customer churn and decreased market value.

Cybersecurity is not a problem for a single company, but generally it affects entire supply chains; suppliers, vendors, and business partners can pose supply chain risks to companies. Supply chain attacks, third-party breaches, and supply chain dependencies can compromise the integrity, availability, and confidentiality of products and services. Through supply chain disruptions, they have a direct impact on customers, leading to identity theft, fraud, and financial harm. Breaches involving customer data can erode trust, damage relationships, and result in customer attrition, which is devastating for companies operating in highly competitive markets. The consequences of lost customer trust are usually perceived in a long term, as trust lost is difficult to regain. All the cybersecurity incidents can have long-term repercussions for companies, including increased insurance premiums, loss of investor confidence, and difficulty in attracting and retaining talent. Addressing cybersecurity risks requires ongoing investment, resources, and commitment to cybersecurity best practices (Bécue et al., 2021). The importance of proactive cybersecurity measures, risk management strategies, and incident response preparedness to mitigate the impact of cyber threats on business operations and resilience should be recognized by managers at all levels of hierarchy, especially in the context of the further development of the Industry 4.0 concept and its components. One of the possible directions for developing Industry 4.0 and dealing with contemporary challenges is the concept of Industry 5.0.

Since each of the first three industrial revolutions was powered by groundbreaking new technology: the power of the steam engine, the efficiency of the assembly line, and the processing speed of the computer a shift is needed. The early industrial eras were known as "revolutions" because the technologies that powered them revolutionized business and production.

The fourth industrial revolution, Industry 4.0, is driven by intelligent technologies. It underpins all Industry 5.0 developments and, by definition, consists of nine key pillars: additive manufacturing, augmented reality, autonomous robots, Big Data analytics, cloud connections and computing, cybersecurity, horizontal and vertical integration of systems, Internet of Things (IoT), simulation, and digital twin.

The fifth industrial revolution is different as it does not focus on technology. Its central pillars are the following concepts (Paschek et al., 2022): Human-centric industry puts human needs and interests at the center of the production process. Instead of asking what employees can do with new technology, Industry 5.0 asks what technology can do for employees. While robots are tireless and precise, they are literal and lack the ability to think critically and creatively about their human partners. In this context, Industry 5.0 does not represent the next industrial revolution, but rather contributes to the development of Industry 4.0 technologies by strengthening the collaboration between humans and robots. With Industry 5.0, the nine pillars of Industry 4.0 have been expanded to include the pursuit of putting human creativity and well-being at the heart of industry to combine the speed and efficiency of machine technologies with the ingenuity and talent of human counterparts. This may be the consequence of the focus on well-being and health issues initiated by the health crisis caused by the COVID-19 pandemic. Balancing industry and economy with social needs Industry 5.0 becomes even more sustainable.

Sustainable industry helps businesses reduce their impact on the environment by developing circular economy processes. Other sustainability changes include reducing energy consumption, greenhouse gas emissions and waste, and avoiding the depletion and degradation of natural resources. Sustainability also means balance and resilience. The resilient industry has a high degree of robustness. It is well-armed with anti-disruption mechanisms and capable of supporting critical infrastructure in times of crisis. The pandemic has highlighted industry vulnerabilities and the importance of greater agility and resilience in supply chains and other production components.

With Industry 5.0, value-driven initiatives overlap with Industry 4.0 technology transformations to enable more seamless interaction between humans and machines. The technologies that enable such interactions are the following (Coelho et al., 2023):

- Human-machine interactions can be customized using built-in sensors, actuators and machine learning technologies to facilitate the adaptation of collaborative robots.
- Human/robot collaboration based on artificial intelligence is being developed to reduce waste, increase compliance with the principles of sustainable development, and increase the efficiency of the use of invested resources.
- Advanced data management and analytics systems use artificial intelligence and machine learning to minimize waste and inefficiency and optimize human talent.
- Simulation models and digital twins minimize wear and tear on real systems and simplify learning and efficiency for human users. This allows for maximum innovation and creativity with minimal operational risk.
- Collaborative robots and experience-based tools such as virtual reality (VR) can help companies double the efficiency of intelligent automation and the creativity and problem-solving skills of their human/robot partners.

Implementation of the technologies listed above creates the conditions for the so-called factory of the future, which is supposed to bring the long-term benefits. The long-term benefits of adopting Industry 5.0 are aligned with socially and environmentally oriented core values, for example, better talent attraction and retention, greater energy savings, and greater overall resilience. Each year, companies have a harder time attracting and retaining the skilled and talented workers they need to compete. When workers are simply machine operators, they lack the challenge and creative input that stimulate development. Industry 5.0 principles and technologies provide a more progressive and interesting work environment, which can help to increase employee satisfaction and loyalty. Social aspects are crucial in Industry 5.0, along with environmental solutions. In the business world, sustainable practices are no longer an option, but an expectation of stakeholders. This applies especially to energy- and resource-intensive industries. A prospective business with sustainable development will be more attractive to potential investors, employees, and consumers. Adopting Industry 5.0 practices will improve the economic performance of the industry while ensuring environmental sustainability.

Industry 5.0 is a solution responding to contemporary challenges. One of them is the ability to respond to disruptive changes such as trade wars, pandemics, and climate impacts, which have become an essential part of running a business. Industry 5.0 technologies play an important role in developing industry agility and resilience through data collection, automated risk analysis, and improved security.

Adopting Industry 5.0 as a complement to Industry 4.0 can significantly expand the workforce. In particular, Industry 5.0 brings highly skilled workers and collaborative robots (cobots) to work side by side, increasing the value each brings to production. Unlike autonomous robots, which work independently once programmed, collaborative robots are designed to respond to human commands and actions. Cobots are equipped with AI-powered sensors, actuators, and controllers that allow them to work alongside humans in a safe and non-intrusive manner. The circuits are versatile, easily programmable, safe, and intuitive to use. The cobot-human relationship is synergistic, in which the innate strengths of both humans and machines are combined to accomplish specific tasks or processes; however, it requires a specific approach to management. There are numerous challenges emerging from human-robot interaction, and managing such mixed teams is a challenge for contemporary managers. Yet, collaboration between humans and cobots can help unlock innovation in many industries, including designer fashion and the automotive industry. The automotive sector was an early adopter of co-bot technologies, using them as key components in assembly lines. By automating repetitive and hazardous tasks such as welding, assembly, and painting, humans are freed up to participate in more complex tasks in addition to operating and maintaining robots, including quality assurance tasks.

The integration of cobots and humans brings with it the potential to personalize and customize goods at an industrial level. While cobots perform repetitive tasks with high efficiency and predictable efficiency, humans can oversee the process to ensure that real-time configuration requests are understood and implemented.

The transition to Industry 5.0 starts with resource management: good planning, solid strategies, open and inclusive communication, and a solid foundation for Industry 4.0.

2.2.2 Resources Management

The basic problem in resource management is achieving a balance between demand and available resources. Classically, demand is unlimited, and size and access to resources are limited. These characteristics largely determine resource management, as they require resolving the conflict between meeting requirements (customer service) and rational use of resources (cost minimization).

The conflict between the degree of resource consumption and the degree of fulfillment of requirements has the nature of a transactional relationship (trade-off) and is universal, i.e., it applies not only to organizations, but can be interpreted much more broadly, in relation to the economy or even humanity. The more resources humanity uses for its development, the fewer opportunities it will have to meet its needs, which is reflected in the so-called iron principle of economics, according to which, due to the limited amount of available resources, the size of the human population and the possibilities of meeting its needs are limited (Malthaus, 1925). In opposition to this view stands one of the concepts identified as a paradigm of modern management: the concept of sustainable development.

Naturally, development is an immanent feature of societies, a condition for the survival and development of civilization, on the one hand a determinant, and on the other hand a consequence of phenomena occurring in all fields and areas of human activity. Development is necessary to meet the individual and collective requirements of society, both in the basic (food, shelter) and extended areas. However, to achieve this, development requires power and the involvement of resources of various types, including natural resources. Therefore, we can talk about a kind of mutual dependence, a close connection, because civilization, in order to develop, i.e., meet the needs of humanity, consumes resources, the production of which requires the implementation of specific tasks and processes, which in turn requires the use of resources.

However, the coherence of mutual interdependencies is disturbed by the analysis of the consequences of excessive exploitation of resources, because they determine the existence of humanity, so their consumption significantly limits not only the fulfillment of requirements and needs, but also the possibility of even basic functioning.

Sustainable resource management, in addition to the macroeconomic, global dimension relating to broadly understood natural resources, also has a microeconomic dimension relating to the management of enterprise resources and treating these resources in a sustainable manner, ensuring balance when setting and pursuing economic, social, and environmental goals. The most advanced and complete approach to sustainable development at the microeconomic level is therefore characterized by a sustainable (taking into account economic, ecological, and social) (Hart and Milstein, 2003) and, at the same time, active approach to resource management by ensuring the so-called triple bottom line (Elkington, 1994), enabling enterprises to achieve their strategic goals, and therefore increase their efficiency and development, including improving their competitive position. This approach is the result of the evolution in resource management, ranging from an exploitative approach to the broadly understood resources at the organization's disposal, through recognizing the limitations and needs resulting from the nature of individual resource categories, to conscious and responsible resource management:

■ Primarily, the approach to resource management was focused on exploitation and based on using resources (human and natural) to achieve organizational goals.
■ Afterwards, awareness was awakened and the approach was focused on financial and technical aspects, treating social and environmental aspects as irrelevant.
■ The next step was increasing compatibility and taking into account requirements regarding the protection of the natural environment and social aspects only to the extent imposed by law and for fear of the possible consequences of violating them.

- Compatibility was followed by effective management, incorporating elements of environmental and HR management into the company's strategy to reduce costs and increase efficiency.
- The next step was including resources management into strategic activity and incorporating elements of environmental and HR management into the company's strategy, recognizing their potential as sources of competitive advantage.
- The final stage is focused on promoting ecological solutions and corporate social responsibility in the company and among stakeholders.

The evolution presented was gradual and can be related to the changes in the perception of resources discussed in the previous chapters, as it constitutes a transition from the instrumental treatment of resources in obtaining markets, and thus competitive advantage, to perceiving the role of resources and their development as a development goal and source of competitive advantage. Thanks to resources, competitive advantage can gain a lasting character, and by developing resources, the organization can develop in a lasting (i.e., sustainable) way.

2.2.3   Contemporary Management

The directions in which changes in management are being developed indicate that management will become more complex, requiring high and varied competencies, and simple models will become useless. The key will be harmonization of activities and integration with the environment, orientation on qualitative aspects, searching for balance and a broader context of activities for both individual employees and the organization.

The identified directions result from the variability and dynamics of the complex environment, and, referring to harmony and interdependence with nature, they also take into account issues of sustainable development and the natural environment, as well as social aspects. The term referring to the business aspects of sustainable development is the concept of corporate sustainability (the terms enterprise sustainability and sustainable enterprise are used interchangeably with the term corporate sustainability), defining a business approach that creates long-term value for stakeholders by taking advantage of opportunities and managing risks related to economic, ecological, and social development. This interpretation does not focus on the environmental dimension and resource consumption but on the sustainability of activities and sustainability of development. In a dynamic environment, characterized by constant change, discontinuity of conditions, and functioning of capabilities, it is crucial to develop or obtain such characteristics of the organization (business model) that will allow the continuation and development of the business even in a hyperdynamic (turbulent) environment. In the literature, there is an original definition of business sustainability presented by I. Hejduk and W. Grudzewski, according to which it is the ability of an enterprise to continuous:

■ Learning,
■ adaptation and development,
■ revitalization,
■ reconstruction,
■ reorientation

to maintain a lasting and distinctive position on the market by offering above-average value to buyers today and in the future (in accordance with the paradigm of innovative growth), thanks to the organic variability that constitutes business models and resulting from the creation of new opportunities and goals and responses to them, while balancing the interests of various groups.

This effect can be achieved through continuous access to knowledge and trust, as well as the ability to move the business into new areas, i.e., redefinition, transformation of core activities, and change of the business model. As a consequence, new challenges for management appear, including:

■ make managers' work serve higher goals;
■ embed the ideas of shared values and citizenship into management systems;
■ reconstruct the basic principles of management;
■ eliminate the pathology of formal hierarchy;
■ calm fears by strengthening trust;
■ redesign the means of exercising control;
■ redefine the role of the leader;
■ promote and use diversity;
■ turn the strategy development process into an evolutionary process;
■ reshape the organization and break it into pieces.

Therefore, a change in the management paradigm results in a completely different perception of the management process and a different interpretation of the boundaries of the organization. In the new management paradigm, critical success factors, identified limitations, and barriers are formulated differently. For the traditional paradigm, the crucial aspect was reduction of direct production costs as the main area of management interest, and operations are stable, while for the new paradigm, reduction of indirect costs of the company while improving competitiveness is crucial, and operations are flexible and constantly improved. Moreover, according to the traditional paradigm, product lines are based on one particularly important technology, and characterized by long product life cycles. Managers are treated as decision-makers and subordinates as passive executors of orders; world markets are divided according to geography, with national enterprises dominating domestic markets. In the new paradigm, product lines are based on multifocal technology, and characterized by short product life cycles. Managers are trainers facilitating work, and subordinates are knowledge workers; markets are global, with attention focused on international economic and political structures (Jamali, 2005).

Solutions enabling success and eliminating or minimizing barriers and limitations can be considered elements of a new management paradigm. There is a view in the literature that there are four areas that determine modern management and define its key solution, and they can be presented in the form of the so-called diamond of the four paradigms of a modern enterprise, including trust, knowledge, innovation, and culture/entrepreneurship. In this approach, the four paradigms mentioned complement each other and synergistically strengthen each other, thanks to which they constitute an effective response to the requirements of the modern market environment.

Innovations in this system respond to the challenges related to shortening the product life cycle; knowledge (competences) is an intangible resource that determines obtaining a competitive advantage, enabling continuous improvement; trust and the culture of entrepreneurship allow building a harmonious work environment. In the new economy (Economy 4.0), knowledge, globalization, digital transformation, turbulence, and networking play crucial roles in interacting and creating synergy.

Change is now a typical state and not, as it was interpreted in the classical approach to management, a temporary deviation from the desired state. Therefore, focusing on stabilizing and routinizing management activities is no longer advisable, and management should accept changes and turn them into opportunities to develop the enterprise's business potential.

However, achieving the effect of this balance is difficult, and what is more, there are a number of indications that the state of imbalance may be beneficial for the company, including:

■ mobilization of the organization resulting from the adoption of ambitious (unbalanced with resources) goals,
■ seeking access to external resources (if it is impossible to achieve the adopted goals using one's own means),
■ focusing on intangible resources, shifting the emphasis to skills and competences when identifying gaps in material resources,
■ increasing the ability to seize opportunities in the event of identified resource redundancy.

This also results in an ambiguous definition of expectations towards modern organizations, which on the one hand should be sustainable, and on the other hand, function in unstable conditions (internal and external). As a result, in opposition to the management paradigm previously characterized by classical definitions, the following conclusions can be presented, constituting the basis for the modern management paradigm/paradigms:

■ management is a specific and distinctive feature of each organization,
■ the organization's job is to lead people, not to direct them. Its main goal is to use the specific skills and knowledge of individual employees to achieve an increase in work efficiency,
■ the basis of management should be the values and needs of customers, which influence decisions regarding the distribution of their income. The starting point for working on a management strategy must be information about the values and needs of the company's potential customers,
■ the scope of management is not defined by law. It must be functional and cover the entire process. It is necessary for management to focus on results and actions throughout the entire economic process,
■ management practices relating only to the business sphere will have to be more often defined in functional terms, rather than political ones,
■ the purpose of management is to ensure the expected results resulting from the activities of a given institution. The management process must begin with defining these effects and ensuring the resources necessary

to achieve them. Management is a kind of tool that is intended to ensure that the institution can achieve the intended results in the external environment in which it operates.

The analysis of the presented conclusions leads to the definition of the elements of contemporary management, i.e., the aspects and goals most often mentioned in the context of management, while at the same time allowing for effective functioning in the modern environment. Obtaining specific characteristics depends on available resources and an appropriate approach to management, which in turn determines the general formulation of the contemporary management model.

The task of modern managers must therefore be to creatively search for new solutions that enable functioning in a complex and dynamic environment and to use emerging opportunities (resulting from the development of science and technology) in order to achieve results that can be defined as follows:

■ customer's satisfaction,
■ systemic management,
■ innovative organization,
■ flexibility.

This composition of organizational goals is justified by customer expectations and has been present in management science and practice for years. Striving for a high level of customer service and achieving a competitive advantage by ensuring customer satisfaction, i.e., customer-oriented management, is an approach that has been used for a long time, only the way in which this approach is implemented changes (from focusing on quality, through focusing on logistics and delivery time, to individual, ecological, and socially responsible customer service). Competing in global markets requires various strategies, not only focused on costs but also individualizing services and products, therefore being innovative and flexible. These approaches are based on holistic, comprehensive management and the use of a systemic approach in order to notice, take into account, and benefit not from individual elements of the enterprise, but from the whole as they constitute and the synergy obtained from the combination and linking of elements.

The implementation of the presented objectives requires the adoption of principles determining the selection of management methods, tools, and techniques, including:

- Added value is the basic social obligation of the enterprise,
- Quality, as a fundamental requirement affecting competitiveness,
- Responding to changes in the environment and customer needs,
- Flexibility in communication and action,
- Development of new ideas, use of employees' creativity and enthusiasm,
- Integration of the technology portfolio to achieve a distinctive competitive advantage,
- Creating multifunctional and multidisciplinary teams.

The principles defined in this way refer to both technical and HR, to quality and flexibility, to the product and process, and therefore indicate many directions in which the company should look for sources of competitive advantage.

Management is therefore expected to make full use of the potential resulting from the contemporary environment, and the organization is expected to adapt to the prevailing market conditions. Adjustment is possible thanks to the appropriate approach of managers and the appropriate selection of management methods, techniques, and tools.

The methods should be aligned with specific features of the market. The components of environmental variability are the individual characteristics of the market and the entities present in it, and the conditions resulting from the characteristics of the environment of the enterprise are also important. The market features that determine the level of volatility, and thus turbulence, are:

- market structure,
- demand,
- market fragmentation,
- market attractiveness,
- price awareness,
- fashion,
- bargaining power of buyers,
- product dissemination model,
- market saturation,
- product life cycle.

Depending on the parameters listed above, both the dynamics and the hostility of the market change.

Competition is a natural manifestation of the feature of turbulence, i.e., the hostility of the environment. Depending on the shape of the competitive environment, i.e., how many competitive entities there are, their bargaining power, and their ability to respond to the customer's needs and requirements, the level of customer hostility is determined. A significant aspect determining the hostility of the environment may also be the level of competition, as the method of competition will differ depending on whether the competition concerns, for example, price, quality, delivery cycle, and the availability of substitute products.

Market variability, but also its hostility, depends on customers and their needs, both conscious and unconscious, current and future, as well as on the variability of these needs, their consistency or diversity (in relation to all customers and individual segments), and the requirements for level of service, including price, quality, and delivery cycle.

In addition to competitors and customers, suppliers are an important component of the market and a determinant of variability. Relationships with suppliers, their reliability, and their ability to respond quickly significantly influence the stability and predictability of the market and thus determine the level of turbulence.

However, the level of turbulence is influenced not only by business entities performing specific roles on the market (suppliers, customers, competitors), but also by the wider environment, although not directly related to enterprises, which significantly determines the conditions of their functioning. Important elements contributing to the variability of the environment and its hostility include:

- requirements regarding the preservation/protection of the natural environment,
- legal regulations,
- administrative regulations,
- economic conditions.

Both the way they are formulated and their constancy and stability are important for the level of environmental turbulence.

The changeability of the environment poses tasks and challenges for modern enterprises that are significantly different from those that businesses had to face in previous periods. To cope with the growing dynamics and hostility of both the immediate and distant environment, companies must adapt to the conditions prevailing there. The conditions that have the strongest impact on the way companies operate, according to research conducted by Zhang and Sharifi, are the growing pressure to reduce costs as a competitive platform, as well as the growing pressure resulting from the globalization of competition and the shortening of product development time as a consequence of increased competition. Also important are the variability of product features, the development of technologies (mainly IT and organizational), growing customer requirements regarding quality and logistic service, and environmental protection requirements. The development of niche markets and the speed of market changes are perceived as factors having a medium impact on the need for new organizational solutions, political changes, both in terms of internal and international policy, shortening of the product life cycle, and related. This includes the scope of innovation and the growing demand for individualized products, quantitative changes in customer orders, the speed of competitors' responses to changes appearing on the market, but also changes in production processes, the introduction of information technologies into production technologies, employee expectations, and legal and political pressures. Cultural changes have the lowest impact on the need to develop a new model of enterprise functioning.

Variability also applies to the interior of the company, the chosen competitive strategy, the product range, the processes implemented and the technologies used. Intrinsic components of variability include:

■ number of products (range of assortment),
■ complexity of the products offered,
■ complexity of the processes implemented, including the manufacturing process and planning and design processes,
■ technology stability,
■ possibility of introducing new technologies.

Intensified competition, requirements of suppliers and customers, and regulations of various nature affect the company's decisions regarding the scope of the product range, the technologies used and the organization of processes, therefore the components of variability mentioned above are not independent, they condition each other. The links and interdependencies in contemporary management can be illustrated with a positive feedback loop: changes in the environment (closer and further) lead to changes inside the company (offer, technology).

By generating change, positive feedback leads to system destabilization. Traditionally, stability was considered the desired state, with changes being disruptions, avoided if possible. Nowadays, variability is a factor of success, as long as the changes are introduced at the right time and are effective, i.e. properly selected, and durable, and if they bring the expected result – solving the problem for which they were undertaken.

Therefore, companies must cope with, and even turn to their advantage, variability at various levels, both that which has its source in the functioning and characteristics of entities operating on the market (customers, suppliers and competitors) and in the functioning and characteristics of entities defining environment, such as administrative and legislative bodies, non-governmental institutions (e.g. related to environmental protection) and the general condition of the economy, as well as internal variability regarding the characteristics of the enterprise, including the product range, its breadth, variability, as well as the processes implemented and the technologies used.

The above-presented operating conditions, although they seem demanding, do not constitute a significant limitation for the development of the enterprise, and what is more, they are well-recognized and described in the literature (Cempel, 2008) as features of complex systems, which business organizations undoubtedly are (Cempel, 2008). In their context, as a consequence of accepting the turbulence of the environment, the concept of using the potential for change appears in the literature (Stankiewicz, 2011). This orientation is characterized by the following features (Matejun and Walecka, 2013):

- treating the high complexity and dynamics of the environment as the basic driving force for the key factors in the development of modern organizations: innovation, entrepreneurship, knowledge, scientific and technical progress,
- porous organizational boundaries or even their absence (Grudzewski et al, 2008) and the focus on permanent, partnership relations with various elements of the environment,
- crossing national and cultural borders and even going beyond the material world (e.g., by using the potential of the digital world) in order to look for opportunities for development,
- awareness of the broader impact of the organization on individual levels of the immediate and distant environment, as well as the social responsibility of the activities undertaken by the organization and its partners,

■ treating crises and risks resulting from the impact of external conditions as specific opportunities for the organization to increase its value and improve its position in the environment.

The turbulent nature of the environment is therefore a challenge for the organization, which, once taken, becomes an impulse for development.

Therefore, the literature on the subject does not currently question the planning paradigm, but rather seeks to eliminate the weaknesses of the planning school and looks for new approaches to planning (Romanowska, 2007). The need for planning at the strategic level was empirically demonstrated by the results of research conducted in the USA in July 2009 among members of the Association for Strategic Planning, according to which organizations used strategic planning (Rupik, 2011; Wilson and Eilertsen, 2010):

■ were better prepared for changes related to the crisis,
■ represented more optimistic attitudes towards the near future (occurrence of an increase in revenues, profits, and improvement of the competitive situation over the next 12 months),
■ in response to changes, they adopted offensive rather than defensive attitudes.

However, planning in turbulent conditions requires a specific approach, as shown by the results of other research conducted in April 2009 by McKinsey on a sample of 594 people holding managerial positions. The conclusions from the conducted research indicate the following changes (Rupik, 2011):

■ a more dynamic/changing structure of the new strategic plan (63% of respondents),
■ conducting more/new analyses (61%),
■ shortening the planning time horizon (56%).

Undoubtedly, however, difficulties related to planning in the context of the limited effectiveness of forecasts pose significant challenges to the science of management and define a field of research that is important from the cognitive theory and application point of view. One of the proposals is the so-called searching for a strategic perspective, inspired by Ansoff's concept of "weak signals" and the achievements of the planning school, consisting in searching for a way to rationally build a strategy in an environment that is difficult to forecast by placing emphasis not on the plan as a result of the planning process but on the stage of strategic analysis and scenario planning (Rupik, 2011), because in this approach, strategy is a process, it is dynamic, aimed at maintaining the development and competitive potential of the enterprise in the long term (Gierszewska and Romanowska, 2009).

2.3 Conclusion

The basis for developing the Readiness, Maturity, and Resilience Model, which is the central element of this book, is to define the conceptual base in the context of contemporary management. For this reason, the starting point for further work is the preparation of a Management Excellence Model, which will be the basis for developing a hierarchical maturity model. The original Management Excellence Model was developed in accordance with Hevner's appreciated scientific design methodology (Schumacher et al., 2016), including:

- Analysis of environment and its conditions,
- Analysis of contemporary solutions,
- Analysis of existing models.

Based on the theoretical framework, the design steps were undertaken, including:

(1) Analysis of requirements, followed by the defined list of requirements,
(2) Model design,
(3) Constraints identification,
(4) Recommendations.

The results of the actions (1)–(4) taken are presented in the following sections.

The starting point of the methodology is to determine business needs resulting from the environment. These needs and requirements were determined on the basis of a review of the literature presenting the conditions of contemporary management. The literature review included the achievements of experts as well as publications containing analyses of case studies; therefore, it referred to existing solutions.

The needs are matched with available applied knowledge, which includes available models related to the designed solution. The models of readiness, maturity, and resilience published in the literature are presented and characterized in Chapter 2.

Based on business needs and available applied knowledge, a model is constructed that meets the identified requirements.

Due to the complexity and wide scope of requirements, the development of the model takes place in two stages: general and detailed.

A synthetic approach to the conditions identified requires locating the organization in a broadly understood environment and then defining its elements. Since, an important requirement for modern management is building competencies, a system of values, and the identity of the organization, the Sankt Gallen approach was used to present the Management Excellence Model.

Sankt Gallen's approach is based on a systems approach. It defines three levels of management: normative, strategic, and operational (Ruegg-Sturm, 1998), which distinguishes it from the American approach (in which management has a dual nature – it can be implemented at the strategic and operational level) and the traditional European approach (in which the level is strategic, tactical, and operational). The highest level of management in the Sankt Gallen approach is the normative level. It is a carrier of the owner's vision of running a business, a specific management philosophy. It is expressed in the pursuit of development (continuous improvement) and understanding of both the environment and the interior of the organization. The strategic level is real and includes striving to improve and optimize the functioning of the organization. It assumes changes in the structure of resources, enabling the implementation of the set goals. The operational level includes achieving goals by implementing appropriately selected solutions – expanding or limiting simple and complex resources, or using them more effectively. The characteristic of this model is a holistic perspective, which, by definition, places the organization in its environment, and this environment not only has a market scope, but is also taken into account on a global horizon.

In the Sankt Gallen model, the organization functions in a social, natural, and economic context, which is consistent with one of the currently applicable management paradigms, the sustainable development paradigm. The organization is influenced not only by elements of the immediate, market environment, but also by the distant ones. In the era of globalization, it is difficult to avoid international connections through which the economic and social situation in the world affects the functioning of enterprises (Table 2.9).

Table 2.9 Contemporary Management Characteristics

Requirements	Management Excellence Model
Management framework	
Implementation of systemic approach	An organization is a system functioning in the environment, complex, consisting of elements connected by connections of various nature, implementing defined functions, transforming supplies into products. The system approach will be implemented by taking into account the holistic perspective, openness and complexity of the organization
Implementation of process approach	Process approach results in a dynamic approach to the organization. The process approach will be implemented by taking into account customer requirements, resource management and continuous improvement
Implementation of functional approach	The essence of the functional approach is the thesis that paramount importance in practical activities, they have standards of use and efficient operation of the system. They refer, for example, to: product properties, technological operations, functions performed in the management process and administrative work, to activities constituting any type of service, also to the stages of creative work. The functional approach will be implemented by taking into account the importance of operational management and the efficiency of the system
Implementation of individual approach	An individual, specific approach to each organization consists in: taking into account its individual goals, limitations and potential and individual selection of methods, techniques and tools used in management
Benefits from opportunities	Identifying and benefiting from opportunities is an important aspect in contemporary management, in which capabilities of an organization enable the organization to identify and use opportunities. One of the opportunities is globalization. Globalization – all processes leading to increasing interdependence and integration of states, societies, economies and cultures, resulting in the creation of "one world", a world society. In the economic dimension, globalization mainly consists in the unification of markets and various goods traded on them. This eliminates most of the existing barriers in international trade

(Continued)

Table 2.9 (*Continued*)   Contemporary Management Characteristics

Requirements	*Management Excellence Model*
	By functioning as an open system in a market environment, the organization will be able to take advantage of opportunities emerging around the world
Shares resources and benefits from shared resources	The organization will be assigned features, i.e. readiness for reconfiguration, flexibility and adaptability, i.e. the ability to use resources at its disposal and those available to other enterprises. The ability to integrate, create both permanent and temporary connections (chains, supply networks) will be taken into account.
Seeks for external resources	The organization will be assigned features, i.e. the need for integration and the ability to perceive synergy resulting from cooperation
Strives for ambitious and unbalanced goals	Planning procedures strive for situations in which resources and tasks are balanced, i.e. when declaring goals, it is assumed that their size and scope will be limited by available resources. When setting goals, the organization will assume that its structure is to result from the adopted strategy (taking into account the possibility of obtaining resources, development, integration)
Benefits from diversity	Diversity in management is expressed in diversification, i.e. a strategy in which the organization makes efforts aimed at expanding its area of operation. The effect of diversification may be the development and maximization of the enterprise's development rate, economic use of resources and strengthening of the market position along with increased security. Diversification resulting from the shortening product life cycle, the need to adapt to customer requirements and market variability will be an element of the agility strategy
Organization	
Based on shared ideas and values	Shared ideas create an organization's identity. The organization will be based on values and ideas common to all its members, identity will constitute an important resource of the organization

(Continued)

Table 2.9 (Continued) Contemporary Management Characteristics

Requirements	*Management Excellence Model*
Flexible	Flexibility results from available technologies and the ability to qualitatively and quantitatively adapt the offer (product) to customer requirements. The organization will demonstrate flexibility in terms of structure (variable, reconfigurable and adaptive structure) and process (variable, reconfigurable and adaptive processes).
Reduced formal hierarchy	Hierarchy is the internal structure of an organization, defining the relationships of superiority and subordination between its members. Organizational hierarchy is closely related to organizational structure The formal hierarchy will be limited due to the assumed flexibility and variability of the structure and the adjustment of the structure to the adopted strategy
Manager	
Idealistics	Higher goals in the context of management are non-economic goals, therefore acting for the general good, society and the environment When functioning in its environment, the organization will take into account the concept of sustainable development, caring for the natural environment, social issues, including intergenerational justice and the principles of corporate social responsibility
It strengthens trust between members of the organization, as well as between the organization and its environment	The modern economy is supposed to be innovative and knowledge-based, which requires the use of human/social capital. Its key element is trust Without it, it is impossible to shape norms or establish networks of cooperation. Trust in business is a condition for taking joint action. An important feature of modern enterprises is that they do not operate alone, they create supply chains and networks, structures that are more or less permanent and integrated, but based on cooperation in achieving the goal The manager's task will be to integrate the organization internally and with the environment by building lasting relationships based on trust, transparent values and goals

(Continued)

Table 2.9 (*Continued*) Contemporary Management Characteristics

Requirements	*Management Excellence Model*
Leader	Leadership can occur in both formal and informal groups. Leadership means striving to achieve common goals (conscious or not) for both parties in this relationship. The leadership relationship is not based on imposing one's own solutions, as in the case of power. The relationship between a leader and his followers is usually based on the voluntary recognition of an individual as a leader. The manager will fulfill the role of leader thanks to the internal trust she/he builds in the organization
Benefits from knowledge	Knowledge builds competences and is a flexible and reconfigurable resource enabling the virtualization of an organization operating in a knowledge-based economy. The manager's role will be to use the knowledge of employees to introduce changes in the organization (reconfigure resources) to use resources, the organization will be assigned the feature of intelligence
Is a coach	Coaching should be treated as a system of organizational functioning that enables optimal use of employee potential, promotes knowledge management in the organization, and is the basis for building a learning organization. It is a process designed to help achieve better results. The manager's role will be to support the learning process and acquiring competences
Creatively seeks for new solutions	Creative search for solutions is one of the elements of the systemic approach. Systems engineering uses many creative thinking (problem solving) methods. The manager's role will be to use the potential of the organization's interior and environment to solve emerging problems in an individualized manner, specific to a given organization

(Continued)

Table 2.9 (*Continued*) Contemporary Management Characteristics

Requirements	Management Excellence Model
Approach to customers	
The values and needs (actual and potential) of customers determine management	Focusing on customer values and needs requires continuous communication with the business environment, information flow, flexibility (adjustment to customer needs), and concurrent product development
Individual approach to customers	Thanks to communication, information flow and concurrent product development, the approach to customers will be individualized, there are no service patterns, flexibility is assumed, taking advantage of emerging opportunities
Approach to competitors	
Cooperation and competition	Support for subcontractors and suppliers. Cooperation will be implemented by building permanent and temporary relationships in the form of supply chains and networks, while cooperation in one project does not exclude competition in another or at a different level
Sharing resources	The Iacocca model assumes cooperation (cooperation) The ability to integrate and create both will be taken into account, as well as ability to create permanent and temporary connections (chains, supply networks)
Increasing competitive advantage	Building competitiveness is based on constant change, quick response, improved quality and environmental responsibility Obtaining a competitive advantage will constitute the basis for the vision and functioning of the organization

(*Continued*)

Table 2.9 (*Continued*)   Contemporary Management Characteristics

Requirements	Management Excellence Model
Approach to products	
Long lifecycles	A long product life cycle increases the environmental friendliness of the offer and opens up the possibility of innovative offers related to the maintenance and regeneration of the product. These features will be characteristic of the organization's offer
Innovative products	Technological advantage, i.e. broadly understood innovation, is important A long life cycle and flexibility (technological agility) as features of the organization will enable the development of innovative products
Individualized products	Individualizing a product means meeting the individual needs of customers and expressing them with individualized treatment Thanks to communication, information flow and concurrent product development, the approach to customers will be individualized, without service patterns. Flexibility and the use of emerging opportunities are assumed
Approach to processes	
Flexible operations	Flexibility is a feature of the enterprise Flexible operations are a response to environmental variability
Continuous improvement	Continuous improvement is an element of the process approach. Using a process approach, continuous improvement of the organization, products and processes
Innovative processes	The innovativeness of the process results from flexibility, individual approach to clients and the development of innovative new products

(*Continued*)

Table 2.9 (*Continued*) Contemporary Management Characteristics

Requirements		Management Excellence Model
Approach to employees		
Employees (their knowledge, competences) are a key resource of the organization		The issue of competences, and therefore human resources (employees), is crucial. Taking into account human resources (their characteristics) as the basis for excellence
Employees are treated as knowledge workers		The issue of knowledge, and therefore human resources (employees), is crucial. Taking into account human resources (their characteristics) as the basis for excellence
Employee creativity is expected		Creative search for solutions is one of the elements of the systemic approach. Systems engineering uses many creative thinking (problem solving) methods. The employee's role will consist in using knowledge and experience to solve emerging problems in an individualized manner, specific to a given job position
It is recommended to work in teams		Teamwork is an element of the systems approach, according to which it provides a synergistic, enhanced effect. Building permanent and temporary teams (for the needs of a given project) is the basis for agile, flexible organizational structures

The summary characteristics listed cover three layers: the first is the environment layer, and a close environment including suppliers, customers, and competitors is considered. The second is the management layer, while the third is the internal layer, including organization, processes, and products (Figure 2.1).

The Sankt Gallen model (Stachowiak, 2019) is a good basis for developing the Management Excellence Model due to taking into account the complexity of the environment necessary to properly model an organization and also the importance of values and vision (normative level), which also play an important role in management. The premise for using the Sankt Gallen model is a holistic approach to management, presenting the organization not as an isolated entity but rather as an object functioning in the environment, subject to its influence and affecting it to varying degrees and scope, and in the context of achieving agility and taking advantage of opportunities emerging in the environment.

The use of the Sankt Gallen approach is justified precisely because of its connection with the systemic methodology, the presence of a normative level defining the organization's identity and values constituting intangible resources, therefore exhibiting VRIN characteristics and thus ensuring a competitive advantage, but also due to the resignation from the tactical level. This level was traditionally responsible for activities related to the allocation of resources and linking resources to tasks, but currently such allocation is dynamic, so it seems advisable to transfer it to the operational level.

Due to its complexity and descriptive nature, the Management Excellence Model will be presented from two perspectives.

The first one is external, exogenous in nature and presents an organization in an environment in which there are separate levels (so-called spheres) of the environment, including: society, the natural environment, the

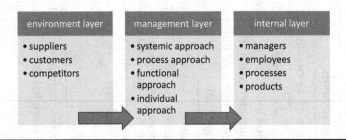

Figure 2.1   The framework of the Management Excellence Model development.

technological environment, and the economy perceived globally and from a holistic perspective.

The second one shows the concept of implementing the company's vision. There are stakeholders in the environment, including suppliers, competitors, customers, investors, administration, public organizations, media, and employees. Opportunities appear in the spheres of the environment. The strength of the influence of the environment on the organization and of the organization on the environment decreases with distance. External spheres influence the organization to a lesser extent, but they also have less influence on it.

Management is implemented at three levels. At the normative level, it builds the company's identity based on values resulting from the personalities and charisma of managers and employees. Values, identity, and organizational culture are common, intangible resources that constitute a source of competitive advantage (due to their VRIN characteristics). They give the organization the ability to spot opportunities in the environment and constitute the basis for building a strategy. In the detailed internal perspective, values, identity and vision are elements of the normative level that are the basis for formulating the mission, building the organizational culture, and managing the concept, and these determine the strategy.

At the strategic level, the organization's goals are formulated based on the company's vision, including obtaining a competitive advantage as a response to market variability, the ability to adapt to changing conditions, and the use of the environment's potential. The strategy is an individual composition, depending on a defined set of goals. Based on a set of goals, the primary goal of which is to achieve a competitive advantage, the organization configures resources, using its own resources and, if necessary, acquiring external and common resources. Resources at this level are tangible and intangible; they do not constitute a limitation when formulating goals (it is possible to use resources that are not owned by the enterprise); they are flexible and therefore enable the implementation of assumptions and ambitious goals. Resources identify available opportunities, including resource-available opportunities.

Resources are operationally reconfigured to take advantage of opportunities identified as available. The degree and scope of taking advantage of opportunities and meeting customer requirements are controlled in the context of effectiveness and efficiency using individually selected indicators and measures (such as flexibility, costs in relation to individual cost objects and others).

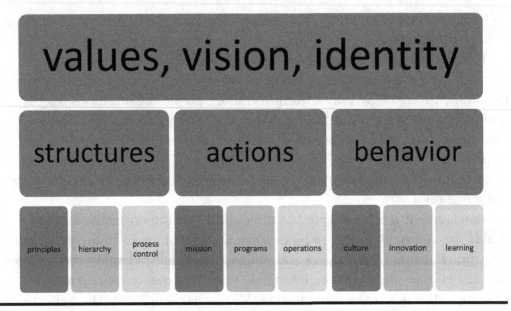

Figure 2.2   The framework of the Management Excellence Model structure.

Therefore, two aspects can be distinguished that characterize the essence of the model from an internal perspective. The first is activities and the resources associated with them; the second is the values created and captured. The spheres of activities and resources play a subordinate role here in relation to creating value for the customer and the ability to capture and maintain it.

In the Management Excellence Model, management includes structures, activities, and behavior (Figure 2.2).

Structures at the normative level do not directly change the structure of the organization in substantive terms, but they indicate the general principles of the organization. At the strategic level, structures, processes and systems are designed, while at the operational level, the main aspect is the control and regulation of the structure. Behavior at the normative level is reflected in the organizational culture; at the strategic level, it includes innovation and higher-order learning, and at the operational level, it includes performance and operational learning. Behavior in the context of higher-order and operational learning corresponds to the already mentioned double-loop learning concept and takes it into account in the defined agility model. The aspect of activities, also horizontal, can be referred to as the classic approach to management, in which the mission is detailed into a policy, i.e., a certain action program, and then its implementation. In the Sankt Gallen model, this system is located at three levels: mission at the normative level, action programs at the strategic level, and activities at the operational level.

The effect of implementing the Sankt Gallen management model is the development of the organization.

The Management Excellence Model was developed to meet the requirements of modern management and make the best use of the potential of the environment. However, the issue of possible barriers or limitations may be subject to discussion. The limitation may be the environment and its legal restrictions, but also competition that reduces the number of potential opportunities and resources available. These conditions balance as feedback between the variability of the environment and the variability of the organization, thanks to which the organization functions in a state of dynamic balance, homeostasis, instead of falling into the trap of positive feedback. The internal limitation is resources, but the essence of modern management is to configure them in such a way that they limit the number of opportunities available for resources as little as possible.

In accordance with the design methodology presented at the beginning of the chapter, the operationalization of the developed model should be considered. The method of carrying out the assessment and implementation guidelines will be presented in the following chapters.

Chapter 3

Readiness, Maturity, and Resilience Model

3.1 Readiness, Maturity, and Resilience Model

The management model presented in the previous chapter assumes that the organization, operating in a changing environment, recognizes the need to adapt to its characteristics. At the same time, it represents a certain set of values and has the resources to achieve the adopted strategic goals. In the model, the main goal is development. The essence of development is moving to more perfect forms. The fundamental concept of development theory is maturity, defined as the organization's ability to systematically improve. The concept of an excellent organization is also interesting in many aspects related to the organization's maturity. The maturity and perfection models have some common features, but there are differences between them (Martusewicz and Szumowiski, 2018). An excellent organization is based, among others, on concepts such as Kaizen (Masaaki, 1986), implemented models of excellence (Jasiulewicz-Kaczmarek and Prussak, 2012), and management models such as the Excellent Innovation Company (Peters and Waterman, 1982). It is also based on the Philosophy of Perfect Management (Krupa, 1999) (orientation towards people, towards the community, leadership, basing activities on trust, proper communication, optimal structure, self-organization, professionalism of each employee and manager, selection of appropriate methods and techniques, attitude pro-ecological) and on the Pyramid of Perfect Management (Kuc, 1999) (at the base of the pyramid are: know, be able, want, be able to, follow, then: planning, strategic planning,

      DOI: 10.4324/9781032688404-3

decision-making, organizing, employing, motivating, distributing, problem solving, monitoring, controlling, and leadership).

Among the excellence models, it is also worth mentioning the RADAR tool used to assess the organization's potential and achievements in the area of EFQM (European Foundation for Quality Management Excellence Model) requirements. It consists of four elements: results, approaches, implementation, assessment, and refinement. They imitate and complement the basic elements of the Deming cycle: plan, do, check, and act by adding specific, more extensive details. RADAR is a dynamic assessment model and an important management tool that provides a foundation to support an organization in dealing with the challenges it faces as it begins to pursue sustainable excellence.

In relation to organizations, maturity should be understood as achieving the highest level of development by striving for perfection. However, it should be remembered that achieving a certain level of maturity does not equate to achieving perfection, because perfection will require continuous improvement (Skrzypek, 2014). There are many models for assessing organizational maturity in the literature on the subject, and they were presented in Chapter 2, together with models of readiness and resilience.

All the three features, readiness, maturity, and resilience, are important for contemporary companies, as they should be ready for the changes and challenges of the contemporary world, mature enough to operate in an organized systemic way, and resilient enough to thrive and prosper in turbulent environments.

To be ready, a company needs to be open, adjustable, and innovative; hence, readiness is best recognized in the context of processes, products and relations with customers.

To be resilient, a company needs to be flexible and able to operate in various conditions; hence, resilience is best recognized in the context of organizations and resources, including human resources and sharing resources to balance them.

To be mature and operate in an organized and systemic way, a company needs to be ready to deal with the changes on the one hand and capable of dealing with them on the other; thus, it needs to be ready and resilient.

To ensure readiness and resilience, and as a consequence, maturity, the Management Excellence Model for responding to exogenous and endogenous changes can be implemented in predefined areas. Table 3.1 presents the areas together with extracted solutions referred to as maturity drivers and maturity aspects, namely readiness and resilience.

Table 3.1 Readiness, Maturity, and Resilience Model

Area	Maturity Drivers	Maturity Aspects
Management framework		
Management principles	Systemic approach Process approach Functional approach Individual approach Benefiting from opportunities Ambitious goals	Readiness: a systematically organized company is ready to implement changes
Organization		
Concept of an organization	Shared values Shared ideas Shared resources Organizational culture Flexible structures Flexible resources	Resilience: a flexible organization with access to shared resources is resilient
Manager		
Manager's profile	Has environmental considerations Has social considerations Sets non-economic goals Trustworthy Charismatics Supports learning Recognizes knowledge of employees Stimulates knowledge acquisition Uses knowledge Uses creative thinking methods Uses problem solving methods	Resilience: a flexible manager open to knowledge acquisition and use makes the organization flexible
Customers		
Customers management	Communication with the business environment Adjusting to the customer's needs Concurrent product development Individualized approach	Readiness: communication with customers makes organizations ready to change

(Continued)

Table 3.1 (*Continued*)   Readiness, Maturity, and Resilience Model

Area	Maturity Drivers	Maturity Aspects
Business environment		
Cooperation and competition	Permanent relationships Temporary relationships Cooperation and competition	Resilience: links and relations with the business environment make the company resilient
Products		
Product management	Environmental friendliness Long lifecycles Innovative products Individual products	Readiness: innovativeness and individualization of products make companies ready for changes
Processes		
Processes management	Flexible operations Innovative processes Continuous improvement	Readiness: innovativeness and individualization of products make companies ready for changes
Employees		
Employees characteristics	Competences Creativity Experience Teamwork	Resilience: the capabilities of employees make the company more resilient

The developed Readiness, Maturity, and Resilience Model includes five levels, arranged from the lowest to the highest, using an intuitive scale extending from the state of lowest maturity (or lack of maturity) to the highest maturity. Maturity related to processes, products, and relations with customers is expressed by innovativeness and openness to changes; hence, it results in readiness, while maturity related to organization, resources, and relations with the business environment (suppliers and competitors) is expressed by flexibility and results in resilience. Readiness and resilience are specific aspects of maturity that synergistically contribute to a company's excellence. Hence, the suggested levels of an organization's maturity are as follows:

- immature,
- of low maturity,
- of medium maturity,
- of high maturity,
- excellent.

The levels are recognized for aspects identified as elements of the Management Excellence model and presented in Table 3.1, namely:

- Management principles,
- Organization,
- Managers,
- Employees,
- Processes (technical resources),
- Products,
- Customers,
- Business environment.

The assessment of maturity can be partial (refer to one only), but it can be holistic as well.

The maturity assessment will be based on the analysis of eight areas, with qualitative leveling terms to characterize them, based on the intuitive use of assessment variables, in accordance with the proposed scale. The scale is based on the perceived level of the descriptive feature and is expressed with the linguistic variables:

- the highest possible level of the feature (HPL),
- high level of feature (HL),
- medium level of the feature (AL),
- low level of the feature (LL),
- lack of any manifestations of a feature (LOF).

A maturity assessment is an internal assessment of the company. The modern endogenous approach, looking through the prism of competences and resources, requires taking into account various perspectives and points of view. Therefore, the maturity assessment should be carried out among managers of all levels and functional areas of the enterprise, which will allow referring to broadly understood resources (tangible and intangible, including competencies). The maturity assessment sheet should reflect the level at which the company represents particular features. The manager, as a stakeholder with knowledge in the given area, is responsible for assessing the level of individual features. At the same time, the completeness of the assessment and its multi-aspect nature require the involvement of not only top management, but also lower-level managers responsible for activities at the operational level. To ensure the reliability of the assessment, it is necessary to present the essence of the maturity features and the method of their interpretation, while the initial activity and training in this area, requiring the specialist knowledge of the trainer, are one-time activities. Conducting a systematic assessment to track how the organization's agility is changing does not require further substantive supervision.

Proprietary tools can be used to conduct an assessment taking into account the indicated structure of maturity characteristics. To increase the utilitarian value of the study, an evaluation sheet was prepared.

The assessment carried out using a table with area descriptions will have a diagnostic dimension. It will provide management with comprehensive, multi-dimensional information regarding individual features and the aggregate level of maturity, in accordance with the scale constituting the Readiness, Maturity, and Resilience Model.

Identification of the maturity level therefore requires a diagnosis of eight areas of the Management Excellence Model. Based on their level of readiness, resilience, and aggregated maturity, an assessment is made. However, the diagnostic dimension does not exhaust the possibilities of the presented model. It can also be used to develop a recommendation constituting an individualized maturity development strategy. Since the defined maturity levels are relatively open, there is no direct indication of the composition (arrangement) of features that are to be represented by the enterprise. The recommended strategy will be individual in nature. A maturity strategy through maturity drivers (properly selected and implemented methods and tools) will help the organization move towards maturity and function effectively in a turbulent environment, while at the same time striving to meet the requirements of stakeholders, standards, specifications, and other regulations to which the company is subject. The specific maturity level (calculated using the procedure presented) and the maturity gaps identified on its basis will provide the basis for recommending actions and selecting methods and tools in such a way as to eliminate or reduce these gaps and, as a result, increase the level of organizational maturity.

3.2 Maturity Assessment

The interpretation of the maturity assessment requires a shift from a qualitative assessment (expressed descriptively) to a quantitative assessment (expressed numerically). Maturity assessment, which is one of the stages of implementation of the design methodology presented at the beginning of the chapter, requires the use of an appropriate tool that would be able to measure the level of characteristics characteristic of maturity in the examined object. The procedure used is based on the approach implemented by the author in many cases to assess maturity. The calculation scheme is based on fuzzy numbers, and basic calculations are used to integrate individual results into an aggregated holistic assessment.

The most important issue in assessing maturity is that it is determined by criteria that should be assessed descriptively, using linguistic variables. The use of linguistic variables involves the use of fuzzy variables, which are the mathematical representation of linguistic variables. The use of fuzzy logic in maturity assessment is also supported by the fact that it is very often used in decision-making (financial, management, etc.) and in expert systems.

The procedure used for this assessment is based on the use of linguistic variables and linguistic values transformed into triangular fuzzy numbers in the fuzzification process. The fuzzy numbers obtained as a result of the evaluation procedure are aggregated into a weighted fuzzy medium using the method of eliminating max-min pairs. The obtained result, which is a fuzzy number, is transformed back into a linguistic value so that the evaluation result is easy to analyze. The Euclidean distance method is used for transformation.

Triangular fuzzy numbers and a fuzzy organizational maturity index can be used to assess maturity, or rather, taking into account the structure and genesis of the developed maturity model, to assess organizational maturity in the context of agile management. Application of elements of fuzzy set theory (Piegat, 2013) in management, including: for assessing the maturity of supply chains (Lin, 2003) or for measuring the maturity of production units Shane (2000) is justified by the difficulties in formulating the assessment on a numerical scale. For this reason, fuzzy maturity measures are adapted to assess maturity. This calculation is based on linguistic variables and linguistic values, transformed into triangular fuzzy numbers in the fuzzification process. The fuzzy numbers obtained as a result of the feature evaluation procedure are aggregated into a weighted fuzzy medium using the max-min pair elimination method. The obtained result, in the form of a fuzzy number, is transformed back into a linguistic value in the defuzzification process, so that the evaluation result is easy to analyze. The Euclidean distance method is used for transformation.

The Aggregated Assessment of the Level of Readiness, Maturity and Resilience, in accordance with the concept included in the Management Excellence Model, requires determining the components of assessments for individual generic maturity features and then, based on the identification of the number of features with a medium or higher rating, drawing conclusions regarding the assessment of the overall social (aggregated).

The presented procedure is based on the assumption that all maturity features are equivalent, and the level of maturity is evidenced by their joint and synergistic occurrence at least a medium level. The very occurrence of a feature may be spontaneous, unintentional, or accidental and unconscious, and in such a situation, it is difficult to refer to excellent management. The transformation of agile behaviors into company routines is expected, but it must come from their purposeful organization.

3.2.1 Striving for Excellence: Maturity Drivers Recommendation

The maturity diagnosis is valuable for the company, but the recommendation of actions leading to increasing the level of maturity has a greater utilitarian value.

The procedure contains subsequent steps and decision rules; therefore, it has the characteristics of an expert system – it uses the Management Excellence Model as a base for minimizing maturity gaps, and it conducts inferences based on built-in decision rules and using the available knowledge database.

The concept of maturity assessment was presented in the previous section in both aggregated and decomposed terms. The next steps of the procedure are to define an initial and dedicated maturity development strategy. In the Management Excellence Model presented in Chapter 2, the development of maturity through the acquisition of maturity features is a result of implementing specific tools/methods/approaches. Based on the determined maturity gap, it is crucial to select maturity drivers to fill this gap by acquiring or strengthening the underrepresented feature.

The presented set of recommendations includes alternative and complementary solutions to fill specific maturity gaps, including a recursive loop to take into account all maturity characteristics subject to assessment.

The first stage of the procedure is to define a set of references that create an initial strategy for increasing maturity. The initial development strategy includes a compilation of drivers, excluding those appropriate for the elemental feature represented at the highest possible level. They are ranked from those requiring urgent implementation – due to the lowest level of the feature they concern, to those less urgent, related to features whose level is rated relatively highest.

The next stage is to adapt the strategy to the individual conditions of the enterprise. This action will be carried out by using a filter system that includes the following filters:

■ presence of a solution,
■ adequacy of a solution,
■ availability of a solution.

The first filter eliminates solutions already used (implemented in the enterprise). The filter is implemented through an interview with the company's management, which includes information about available resources and applied solutions. Thanks to its use, a set of solutions not used by the company is defined.

The second filter (adequacy) allows to select a solution appropriate for a given sector, size and nature of the enterprise. The filter is implemented through consultations with experts to match appropriate solutions to the profile (requirements and limitations) of the sector. Thanks to its use, a set of solutions suitable for a given enterprise is defined.

The third filter (availability) allows to select available solutions. The availability criterion may be the cost of the solution or the availability of suppliers. The third filter requires consultation with the procurement department and the finance department as units that have knowledge of the supplier market and access to data on available funds and possible investment opportunities. Thanks to its use, a set of media recommended for implementation is defined.

Ultimately, after carrying out the entire procedure, the company receives a set of solutions selected to fill or minimize the identified maturity gaps. The implementation of the recommendations will, in principle, result in closing the gap and therefore increasing the level of maturity; however, an immediate improvement in the enterprise's parameters cannot be expected. The observable effect depends on the intensity of isolated problems and selected solutions, as well as the degree and scope of their implementation.

3.3 Case Study: Readiness, Maturity, and Resilience of a Paper Industry Representative

The diagnosis of Readiness, Maturity, and Resilience was conducted at a production company in the paper industry. The company is classified as medium (number of employees between 50 and 249) and operates in Poland, but it conducts business on an international scale, selling its products to customers worldwide.

The structure of a company is simple; it comprises functional departments led by managers.

The decision to diagnose the company's readiness, maturity, and resilience was taken after a shift at the top management level.

The diagnosis was conducted during a workshop meeting in July 2023. Prior to the diagnosis, the Management Excellence Model and concept of maturity were briefly discussed. The diagnosis procedure was explained, and the research tool was characterized. The results of the diagnosis were presented to the managers and explained.

The diagnosis of the level of maturity was carried out in accordance with the methodological assumptions presented in the first chapter; managers at all levels were asked to answer questions regarding the level of individual aspects of maturity. The interview was conducted with 18 managers, so the diagnosis can be considered complete as a full picture of the organization was obtained.

The study used a questionnaire consisting of two parts. In the first one, the questions concerned the experience of managers in their position, in the sector, and in the company. The aim was to determine the level of knowledge about the company and its specifics. In the second one, managers were asked to relate statements directly related to the level of maturity in the areas that determine excellent management.

Based on the answers to the questions in the first part of the research sheet, the levels of knowledge and experience of the respondents were determined. The measure of experience was the time in which the following ranges were distinguished:

- up to 5 years,
- more than 5 but less than 10 years,
- more than 10 but less than 20 years,
- more than 20 years.

Most respondents have been working professionally for more than 10 years but less than 20 years (78% of respondents). Therefore, they have some professional experience. However, it can be assumed that the management staff of the examined company is relatively young.

In addition to professional experience, knowledge of the sector is important. The experience of managers related to the sector represented by the enterprise (paper industry) is evenly distributed in three ranges: less than 5 years (28%), more than 5 years and less than 10 (39%), more than 10 years and less than 20 years (33%). Experience resulting from work in other sectors provides a good basis for a reliable assessment of enterprises – from different perspectives, the possibility of relating and comparing different business environments. From the point of view of assessing the company's maturity, this is a favorable situation.

Knowledge of the company and its specific conditions was also considered important, and therefore respondents were asked about their cooperation with the assessed company.

The respondents' answers show that their experience in the sector is slightly greater than their experience in the company. However, considering that more than half of the respondents have been working in the company for over 5 years (5–10 years – 50%, 10–20 years – 17%), their knowledge about the organization is sufficient to carry out the planned assessment.

From the point of view of the nature of the study, it was justified to conduct it among people performing managerial functions, i.e., those who make decisions, plan, and have resources. Therefore, each of the respondents has some experience working in a managerial position – 56% of respondents have managerial experience shorter than 5 years, 39% have been working as managers for 5–10 years, and 5% are the most experienced managers with more than 10 years of experience at the position.

The respondents' experience in managerial positions is at a medium level, which can be considered beneficial from the point of view of organizational agility – managers have not yet acquired operational routines and are open to new management concepts.

Taking into account the respondents' experience in the assessed categories, their agility assessment was assigned weights reflecting their professional experience in the sector, enterprise, and managerial position, determined as the medium of the ratings obtained in the assessed categories, where for experience at the lowest level (less than 5 years) 0.25 points were given, in the 5–10 range 0.5 points were granted, and for 10–20 years of experience 0.5 points were granted, while for the highest level (over 20 years of experience) 1 point was given. The summary of assessments is given in Table 3.2.

The weights of experience and knowledge associated with individual respondents will be included in the presentation of the results of the maturity assessment conducted among respondents in the second part of the questionnaire.

Table 3.2   Respondents Experience

Respondent Manager (RM)	Professional Experience	Experience in the Sector	Experience in the Company	Experience at the Position	Weight of Experience (Mean)
RM 1*	0.75	0.5	0.5	0.25	0.5
RM 2	0.75	0.25	0.25	0.25	0.38
RM 3	0.5	0.5	0.5	0.25	0.44
RM 4	0.75	0.75	0.75	0.25	0.63
RM 5	0.75	0.25	0.25	0.5	0.44
RM 6	0.75	0.25	0.25	0.5	0.44
RM 7	0.75	0.5	0.5	0.25	0.5
RM 8	0.5	0.5	0.25	0.25	0.38
RM 9	0.75	0.75	0.75	0.5	0.69
RM 10	0.75	0.25	0.25	0.5	0.44
RM 11	0.5	0.5	0.5	0.25	0.44
RM 12	0.75	0.5	0.5	0.5	0.56
RM 13	0.75	0.5	0.5	0.25	0.5
RM 14	0.75	0.75	0.5	0.75	0.69
RM 15	0.5	0.25	0.25	0.25	0.31
RM 16	0.75	0.75	0.5	0.5	0.63
RM 17	0.75	0.75	0.75	0.5	0.69
RM 18	0.75	0.75	0.5	0.25	0.56

* Respondent Manager 1: RM 1, numbers assigned in a random way.

3.3.1 Diagnosis Results

The main aim of the study was to assess the identified areas of maturity. A five-point scale was used for the evaluation, including:

- the highest possible level of the feature (HPL),
- high level of the feature (HL),
- medium level of the feature (AL),
- low level of the feature (LL),
- lack of any manifestations of the feature (LOF).

The study obtained ratings for all characteristics indicated by all RMs. The diagnosis can therefore be considered complete.

The research results are presented in charts profiled for individual elementary agility features; the number of indications for the feature levels specified in the assessment methodology is presented (Table 3.3).

The assessments of individual maturity aspects determined by the RM presented in the summary are varied. However, it is worth noting the small number of answers indicating the lack of manifestations of the feature. It is also interesting that the medium level of features was relatively rarely indicated, but high and highest ratings are often indicated. This may prove the high assessment of the company in the eyes of its employees and the actual implementation of the company's declaration regarding development and improvement. Natural discrepancies between the assessments can be observed, which may indicate differences in the perception of maturity characteristics depending on the perspective (department, function, management level). The aim of the study was to diagnose the maturity of the company from an internal (endogenous) perspective, but without distinguishing or discriminating against any of the functional areas or levels in the hierarchical structure; therefore, despite the observed discrepancies, the obtained ratings are not subject to trimming.

After carrying out the partial assessment, it is possible to aggregate its results and present the assessment of maturity and maturity aspects, namely readiness and resilience.

The aggregation procedure was presented in the previous section. It is based on transforming linguistic grades into fuzzy numbers and calculating the medium grade.

To obtain an aggregated grade, the transposition of verbal grades into numerical grades is required. The presented methodology proposes the

Table 3.3   Research Tool With Responses of Managers (RMs)

Area	Response	Number of RMs
Business environment: cooperation and competition based on temporary and permanent relationships and building supply networks	The highest possible level of the feature	1
	High level of feature	12
	Medium level of the feature	3
	Low level of the feature	2
	Lack of any manifestations of the feature	
Manager's profile: idealistic and flexible manager open to knowledge acquisition and use	The highest possible level of the feature	8
	High level of feature	3
	Medium level of the feature	6
	Low level of the feature	1
	Lack of any manifestations of the feature	
Employees: competencies of employees, their creativity, experience, and ability to work in teams	The highest possible level of the feature	3
	High level of feature	8
	Medium level of the feature	4
	Low level of the feature	2
	Lack of any manifestations of the feature	1
Processes: flexible processes, continuously improved and innovative	The highest possible level of the feature	
	High level of feature	7
	Medium level of the feature	6
	Low level of the feature	5
	Lack of any manifestations of the feature	

(Continued)

Table 3.3 (*Continued*)   Research Tool With Responses of Managers (RMs)

Area	Response	Number of RMs
Products: innovative, with a long lifecycle, environmentally friendly, and individual	The highest possible level of the feature	3
	High level of feature	8
	Medium level of the feature	4
	Low level of the feature	3
	Lack of any manifestations of the feature	
Management: supporting employees, benefiting from their knowledge, and being creative and idealistic	The highest possible level of the feature	5
	High level of feature	7
	Medium level of the feature	4
	Low level of the feature	2
	Lack of any manifestations of the feature	
Organization: flexible and shared resources, with a built-in culture	The highest possible level of the feature	10
	High level of feature	1
	Medium level of the feature	7
	Low level of the feature	
	Lack of any manifestations of the feature	
Customers: approach to customers based on communication, individual and flexible	The highest possible level of the feature	3
	High level of feature	9
	Medium level of the feature	2
	Low level of the feature	3
	Lack of any manifestations of the feature	1

use of fuzzy numbers, which allows the assessment to be aggregated into a medium and a weighted medium (taking into account the weight reflecting the experience of experts). The aggregation was performed in two variants: in one, the medium of experts' ratings was determined; in the other, weights were determined for experts, assessing their experience (in a position, in a sector, in an enterprise).

Fuzzification of variables (assessments of the level of maturity) was carried out using triangular fuzzy numbers according to the scheme:

■ the highest possible level of the feature (HPL): 0,67; 0,84; 1,0
■ high level of feature (HL): 0,5; 0,67; 0,84
■ medium level of the feature (AL): 0,34; 0,5; 0,67
■ low level of the feature (LL): 0,14; 0,34; 0,5
■ lack of any manifestations of feature (LOC): 0,0; 0,14; 0,34

In the next step, the mean ratings for the maturity areas are determined.

The fuzzy average of individual assessments is determined based on the formula:

$$\text{RWDO}_j = \frac{\sum_{i=1}^{n} R_i}{n}$$

where, RWDO_j – Fuzzy Maturity index of an area, j – Number of characteristics, R_i – Level of the area i, i – Number of the area, n – Number of areas.

The study determines the level of individual features in order to define the level of organizational maturity.

The membership function of this fuzzy variable can be defined as follows:

$$f_{\text{RWDO}}(y) = \sup.\min.\left\{ f_{R_i}(R_i), i = 1...n, y = \frac{\sum_{i=1}^{n} R_i}{n} \right\}$$

for each $i=1, 2,..., n$, f_{R_i} is the membership function of the fuzzy number R_i.

The procedure for eliminating max-min pairs for calculating the function includes the following steps:

1. Limit the range of the membership function to finite numbers α_1, α_2, ... α_n in the range <0,1>.
2. For each α_j, find the appropriate range of feature coefficients $[a_i, b_i]$ and the range of their appropriate weights $[c_i, d_i]$, with $i = 1...n$.
3. Find the maximum value of a_1 such that $a_1 \geq a_i$, the maximum value of b_1 such that $b_1 \geq b_i$, and the minimum value of a_n such that $a_i \geq a_n$, and the minimum value of b_n such that $b_i \geq b_n$.
4. For the minimum value $\{f_l\}$, select c_1 as the weight appropriate for a_1 and d_n as the weight for a_n. For the maximum value $\{f_U\}$, select d_1 as the weight corresponding to b_1 and c_n as the weight for b_n.

$$f_u = f(w_1, w_2 ... w_n) = \frac{\sum\limits_{i=1}^{n} b_i W_i}{\sum\limits_{i=1}^{n} W_i}$$

$$f_L = f(w_1, w_2 ... w_n) = \frac{\sum\limits_{i=1}^{n} a_i W_i}{\sum\limits_{i=1}^{n} W_i}$$

5. Connect a_1 and a_n and their respective weights c_1 and d_n according to the scheme:

$$\min\{f_L\} \, a' = \frac{(a_1 c_1 + a_n d_n)}{(c_1 + d_n)}$$

$$w' = c_1 + d_n$$

$$c' = d' = w'$$

6. Connect b_1 and b_n and their respective weights d_1 and c_n according to the scheme:

$$\max \{f_U\}\, b' = \frac{(b_1 d_1 + b_n c_n)}{(d_1 + c_n)}$$

$$w' = d_1 + c_n$$

$$c' = d' = w'$$

7. Eliminate a_1, a_n, c_1, and d_n, replacing them with a' and w'. Eliminate b_1, b_n, d_1, and c_n, replacing them with b' and w'. Enter the newly calculated values among the existing ones.
8. Repeat steps 1–4 $(n-1)$ times, the last a' and b' will be the solution for j. Repeat the procedure for each j.

To facilitate the interpretation of the result, the assessment was defuzzified, i.e. its linguistic value was restored. The defuzzification procedure was based on the determination of the Euclidean distance and is described in Section 4.3.

The index is translated into a descriptive maturity level. The calculation of the Euclidean distance between a given fuzzy number and each of the fuzzy numbers representing the range of natural language expressions is implemented, as it is the most intuitive, and the others are difficult to implement (Lin, 2003). The following formula is used to calculate the Euclidean distance:

$$d\left(\text{FMI}, JN_i\right) = \sqrt{\left(\sum_{x=1}^{p} f_{\text{MI}}(x) - f_{\text{Ni}}(x)\right)^2}$$

where, N_i is the natural language expression (assessment of the feature), x is the point at which distance is measured, i is the number of the point, p is the number of points, and $f_{\text{MI}}(x)$ is the value at point x for which the natural expression is identified. $f_{\text{Ni}}(x)$ is the distance at every x point.

The result of the procedure is also given in Table 3.4.

When the assessment of respondents managers is considered there are slight differences in maturity assessment, as evidenced in Table 3.5.

The maturity concept is based on readiness and resilience. Concluding on maturity is based on an analysis of readiness and resilience assessment (Table 3.6).

Based on the analysis of the results presented in the table, the resilience of the organization is higher than its readiness. An organization is resilient at a high level, while its readiness is assessed as medium.

Table 3.4   Maturity Assessment Results

Area	Mean of RMs' Assessment	Interpretation
Business environment	(0,44; 0,61; 0,78)	High level
Manager's profile	(0,50; 0,67; 0,84)	High level
Employees	(0,43; 0,59; 0,76)	Medium level
Processes	(0,35; 0,52; 0,69)	Medium level
Products	(0,43; 0,61; 0,77)	Medium level
Management	(0,47; 0,64; 0,81)	High level
Organization	(0,53; 0,70; 0,86)	High level
Customers	(0,42; 0,60; 0,76)	Medium level

Table 3.5   Weighted Maturity Assessment Results

Area	Weighted Mean of RMs' Assessment	Weighted Interpretation
Business environment	(0,43; 0,60; 0,77)	Medium level
Manager's profile:	(0,48; 0,66; 0,82)	High level
Employees:	(0,41; 0,58; 0,75)	Medium level
Processes	(0,34; 0,51; 0,68)	Medium level
Products	(0,42; 0,59; 0,76)	Medium level
Management	(0,46; 0,63; 0,80)	High level
Organization	(0,52; 0,69; 0,85)	High level
Customers	(0,41; 0,58; 0,75)	Medium level

Table 3.6 Readiness and Resilience Assessment Results

Aspects of Maturity	Area	Interpretation	Weighted Interpretation
Resilience	Business environment	High level	Medium level
	Manager's profile:	High level	High level
	Employees	Medium level	Medium level
	Organization	High level	High level
Readiness	Management	High level	High level
	Processes	Medium level	Medium level
	Products	Medium level	Medium level
	Customers	Medium level	Medium level

The linguistic value closest to the determined index corresponds to the level of the assessed process. The assessments of individual features are used to determine the aggregated maturity level. Thus, aggregated maturity level calculation requires the determination of evaluation for maturity features and then calculation, based on the identification of a number of medium- or higher-rated features, drawing conclusions about the overall (aggregated) assessment.

Aggregating the ratings at the level of elementary features made it possible to identify 4 features at a high level and 4 at an average level, while taking into account the weighted ratings gives 5 average and 3 high ratings. The initial assessment of the organization's maturity provides grounds for defining it as average.

To calculate the overall maturity of an organization, the Fuzzy Maturity Index is calculated with the formula:

$$FMI_j = \frac{\sum_i^n MF_i}{8}$$

where, FMI_j (Fuzzy Maturity Index) of j-process, j-area index (j=1.8 for maturity areas), MF_i – level of the individual area's maturity i.

Calculations made indicate that the Maturity Index weighted with the experience of the respondents (0,43; 0,6; 0,77) is slightly lower than the one considering responses at an equal level (0,45; 0,62; 0,78). The difference is

Table 3.7 Ranking of Maturity Areas

Area	Mean of RMs' Assessment	Weighted Mean of RMs' Assessment	Ranking
Business environment	(0,44; 0,61; 0,78)	(0,43; 0,60; 0,77)	4
Manager's profile:	(0,50; 0,67; 0,84)	(0,48; 0,66; 0,82)	2
Employees:	(0,43; 0,59; 0,76)	(0,41; 0,58; 0,75)	6
Processes	(0,35; 0,52; 0,69)	(0,34; 0,51; 0,68)	7
Products	(0,43; 0,61; 0,77)	(0,42; 0,59; 0,76)	5
Management	(0,47; 0,64; 0,81)	(0,46; 0,63; 0,80)	3
Organization	(0,53; 0,70; 0,86)	(0,52; 0,69; 0,85)	1
Customers	(0,42; 0,60; 0,76)	(0,41; 0,58; 0,75)	6

not big yet impacts the interpretation of the maturity level, as it indicates a medium instead of a high level of maturity.

To provide feedback on the maturity of the company and suggest improvement actions, a ranking of assessments was prepared (Table 3.7).

The areas ranked the highest are the organization and manager's profile; they are important components of resilience, while the lowest are processes, reflecting the readiness of the company.

Based on the diagnosis of the enterprise's maturity at the level of areas and their elementary features, it is possible to identify maturity gaps and develop a recommendation for maturity carriers to fill the identified gaps and increase the maturity level.

3.3.2 Conclusions and Recommendations

Maturity diagnosis is useful for an enterprise because it indicates the level of maturity areas, readiness level, and resilience level. Moreover, it enables the assessment of the level of organizational maturity.

The assessments determined in the maturity diagnosis and the guidelines presented in the model show that the examined company has an average level of maturity and is a more resilient than ready organization. The average level of maturity is a consequence of the actions taken, including those aimed at continuous development and improvement, but limited by insufficient flexibility and innovativeness of processes.

To develop recommendations for maturity drivers, the gap defined on the basis of the averages of RM assessments was used.

To complete the diagnosis of the enterprise's maturity level, it is necessary to identify the maturity gap. The identified gap should be filled according to the recommendations set out in the Management Excellence Model.

The gap should be filled by applying defined decision rules in the order resulting from the assessment of individual areas, which includes the assessment in the form of a fuzzy and defuzzified average. Since none of the areas was rated as the highest, an improvement process should be implemented for each of them.

Recommendations are presented from the lowest to the highest-rated maturity feature. Adjusting this strategy for the company requires the use of filters. The first is a filter that eliminates drivers already in use. Identifying the drivers used requires knowledge of the company's resources. The best source of data are the company's employees – information on available media was obtained from the interviewed RMs.

In the examined company, the filter eliminated some of the drivers, leaving the recommended composition (Table 3.8).

Table 3.8 Recommendations Based on the First Filter (Presence in Company)

Area	Maturity Drivers	Comments
Management framework		
Management principles	Systemic approach Functional approach Individual approach Benefiting from opportunities Ambitious goals	The process approach was eliminated with the first filter as the company implemented the process approach. Processes are owned by managers and managed with KPIs
Organization		
Concept of an organization	Shared values Shared ideas Shared resources Organizational culture	In the organization, resources are flexible, but only human resources. They are increased and decreased depending on demand. Flexibility of resources determines flexibility of structures and teams.

(Continued)

Table 3.8 (*Continued*)   Recommendations Based on the First Filter (Presence in Company)

Area	Maturity Drivers	Comments
Manager		
Manager's profile	Has environmental considerations Has social considerations Sets non-economic goals Trustworthy Charismatics Supports learning	Driven related to knowledge were eliminated as managers proved to be aware of its knowledge importance, and they are actively promoting knowledge-focused activities
Customers		
Customers management	Communication with the business environment Adjusting to the customer's needs Concurrent product development	Individualized approach was eliminated as the company implemented an individual approach towards customers' needs and expectations
Business environment		
Cooperation and competition	Temporary relationships Cooperation and competition	Permanent relationships as a driver were eliminated as the company has long-term contracts and cooperation with its business partners
Products		
Product management	Environmental friendliness Long lifecycles Innovative products	Individual products are already a part of the company's strategy
Processes		
Processes management	Flexible operations Innovative processes Continuous improvement	No drivers were removed – operations are flexible, but processes are not improved

(Continued)

Table 3.8 (*Continued*)   Recommendations Based on the First Filter (Presence in Company)

Area	Maturity Drivers	Comments
Employees		
Employees characteristics	Competences Creativity Experience Teamwork	No drivers were removed; employees lack creativity and experience; they do not work in teams (which may be caused by high staff fluctuations)

The diagnosed level of maturity was confirmed by a limited number of eliminated (and therefore already implemented) drivers. After applying the first filter, it remains to be decided whether to implement the recommended drivers. At this stage, the second filter is used, related to the adequacy of solutions (in relation to the sector represented by the enterprise and the scope of its activities), and then the third one is related to the company's capabilities (financial resources, time, and possibilities). The use of these filters requires an analysis of the current situation of the company and its confrontation with the adopted strategic assumptions.

The presented case study is illustrative and shows how to practically use the proposed approach. It can be a reference for future users of the assessment, fulfilling an explanatory function, explaining the next steps in the procedure, and how to interpret the assessment.

Summary

The key areas presented in this book include not only readiness, maturity, and resilience but also turbulence, sustainability, and Industry 4.0/5.0. These topics are widely discussed and presented in many books, articles, and presentations. The material presented does not reflect the full knowledge in the areas of readiness, maturity, resilience and contemporary management, though it aims to present a broad perspective, starting from the first works in the field and including the latest works as well.

The theoretical review included in the book can be the inspiration for deepened literature studies to explore the topics, while the practical part could inspire conducting the research to use the methodology/ies presented and benchmark the results.

The topics of readiness, maturity, and resilience are interesting in the context of contemporary business conditions and the challenges contemporary companies are facing, both from an educational perspective and from a utilitarian perspective as well.

The Management Excellence Model and Readiness, Maturity, and Resilience Model presented in this book are universal; they do not refer to any industry or geographical area. As universal, they need to be adjusted/customized, when implemented, with the set of filters suggested.

The case study presented in the book is an illustration on Readiness, Maturity, and Resilience Model implementation, maturity assessment, and improvement recommendation development. The methodology can be used in any organization, as it does not refer to any specific process or structure.

In the contemporary world, it is impossible to decide whether it is better to be ready, mature, or resilient, hence the suggested synergetic compilation of the terms. Let's be ready and resilient while maturing in our roles in the economy and society.

References

Akdil, K. Y., Ustundag, A., & Cevikcan, E. (2018). Maturity and readiness model for Industry 4.0 strategy. In *Industry 4.0: Managing the Digital Transformation*. Springer Series in Advanced Manufacturing (pp. 61–94). Springer. https://doi.org/10.1007/978-3-319-57870-5_4

Akmal, A., Podgorodnichenko, N., Greatbanks, R., Foote, J., Stokes, T., & Gauld, R. (2021). Towards the development of a system-wide quality improvement maturity model: A synthesis using systematic review and expert opinion. *International Journal of Lean Six Sigma, 15*(3), 503–540.

Aldrich, H. E. (1979). *Organizations and Environments*. Englewood Cliffs, NJ: Prentice-Hall, Inc.

Alguliyev, R., Imamverdiyev, Y., & Sukhostat, L. (2018). Cyber-physical systems and their security issues. *Computers in Industry, 100*, 212–223.

Al-Khatib, A. W. (2023). The impact of industrial Internet of things on sustainable performance: The indirect effect of supply chain visibility. *Business Process Management Journal, 29*(5), 1607–1629.

Allen, R., & Toder, F. (2004). A model of organizational recovery. *Journal of Emergency Management, 2*(1), 41–45.

Ambulkar, S., Blackhurst, J., & Grawe, S. (2015). Firm's resilience to supply chain disruptions: Scale development and empirical examination. *Journal of Operations Management, 33*, 111–122.

Amit, R., & Schoemaker, P. (1993). Strategic assets and organizational rent. *Strategic Management Journal, 14*, 33–46.

Anastas, P. T., & Zimerman, J. B. (2003). Through the 12 principles of Green engineering. *Environmental Science and Technology, 37*(5), 95–101.

Andersen, T. J., & Bettis, R. A. (2015). Exploring longitudinal risk-return relationships. *Strategic Management Journal, 36*(8), 1135–1145.

Annarelli, A., & Nonino, F. (2016). Strategic and operational management of organizational resilience: Current state of research and future directions. *Omega, 62*, 1–18.

Ansoff, H. I. (1985). Conceptual underpinnings of systematic strategic management. *European Journal of Operational Research, 19*(1), 2–19.

Arthur, W. B. (1996). Increasing returns and the new world of business. *Harvard Business Review, 74*, 100–109.

Ates, A., & Bititci, U. (2011). Change process: A key enabler for building resilient SMEs. *International Journal of Production Research, 49*(18), 5601–5618.

Ávila-Gutiérrez, M. J., Martín-Gómez, A., Aguayo-González, F., & Córdoba-Roldán, A. (2019). Standardization framework for sustainability from circular economy 4.0. *Sustainability, 11*(22), 6490.

Axelos, K. (2023). *The Game of the World*. Edinburgh: Edinburgh University Press.

Bag, S., Dhamija, P., Luthra, S., & Huisingh, D. (2023). How big data analytics can help manufacturing companies strengthen supply chain resilience in the context of the COVID-19 pandemic. *The International Journal of Logistics Management, 34*(4), 1141–1164.

Baines, T., Ziaee Bigdeli, A., Sousa, R., & Schroeder, A. (2020). Framing the servitization transformation process: A model to understand and facilitate the servitization journey. *International Journal of Production Economics, 221*, 107463.

Barlett, C. P., Simmers, M. M., Roth, B., & Gentile, D. (2021). Comparing cyberbullying prevalence and process before and during the COVID-19 pandemic. *The Journal of Social Psychology, 161*(4), 408–418.

Barney, J. B. (1991). Firm resources and sustained competitive advantage. *Journal of Management, 17*(1), 99–120.

Bartel, C. A., & Rockmann, K. (2024). The disease of indifference: How relational systems provide the attentional infrastructure for organizational resilience. *Strategic Organization, 22*(1), 18–48.

Batz, A., Oleśków-Szłapka, J., Stachowiak, A., Pawłowski, G., & Maruszewska, K. (2020). Identification of Logistics 4.0 maturity levels in Polish companies—Framework of the model and preliminary research. In R. Grzybowska, K. Awasthi, & A. Sawhney (Eds.), *Sustainable Logistics and Production in Industry 4.0: New Opportunities and Challenges* (pp. 161–175). Cham: Springer.

Bécue, A., Praça, I., & Gama, J. (2021). Artificial intelligence, cyber-threats and Industry 4.0: Challenges and opportunities. *Artificial Intelligence Review, 54*(5), 3849–3886.

Bednarczyk, M. (1996). *Otoczenie i przedsiębiorczość w zarządzaniu strategicznym organizacją gospodarczą* (Vol. 128). Kraków: Akademia Ekonomiczna w Krakowie.

Benbasat, I., Dexter, A. S., & Mantha, R. W. (1980). Impact of organizational maturity on information system skill needs. *MIS Quarterly, 4*, 21–34.

Bhamra, R., Dani, S., & Burnard, K. (2011). Resilience: The concept, a literature review and future directions. *International Journal of Production Research, 49*(18), 5375–5393.

Bilgiç, E., & Aydoğan, T. (2023). Investigating the role of organizational culture in the digitalization process: A critical analysis of the literature through co-word analysis in organizational behavior in the digital world. In M. Z. Çögenli (Ed.), *Organization, Business and Management; Business, Technology and Finance*. https://doi.org/10.52305/FAMR4883

Bilgiç, E., Aydin, E., & Aydoğan, T. (2023). Does being more sustainable make firms less manipulative? Understanding the role of corporate sustainability and the COVID-19 crisis in financial manipulation. *Is Ahlakı Dergisi, 16*(2), 40–65.

Black, J. A., & Boal, K. B. (1994). Strategic resources: Traits, configurations and paths to sustainable competitive advantage. *Strategic Management Journal, 15*(S2), 131–148.

Black, J. A., & Boal, K. B. (1994). Strategic resources: Traits, configurations and paths to sustainable competitive advantage. *Strategic Management Journal, 15*(S2), 131–148.

Bluedorn, A. C. (1993). Pilgrim's progress: Trends and convergence in research on organizational size and environments. *Journal of Management, 19*(2), 163–191.

Borys, T. (2013). Dojrzałość człowieka i organizacji. In E. Skrzypek (Ed.), *Dojrzałość organizacji—aspekty jakościowe* (pp. 46–59). Lublin: Katedra Zarządzania Jakością i Wiedzą, Wydział Ekonomiczny, Uniwersytet Marii Curie-Skłodowskiej w Lublinie.

Brews, P., & Purohit, D. (2007). Strategic planning in unstable environments. *Long Range Planning, 40*(1), 64–83.

BS 65000:2014. (2014). *Guidance on Organizational Resilience.* London: British Standards Institution.

British Standard Institute (BSI) (2018). https://knowledge.bsigroup.com/?creative=319090292352&keyword=british%20standards&matchtype=p&network=g&device=c&gad_source=1&gclid=CjwKCAjwkJm0BhBxEiwAwT1AXJbDugeIzTa4PIs7RZsOjDpCXs7hfc1tJQeJPNDBIxcPfRoyfSfQHBoCi8wQAvD_BwE&gclsrc=aw.ds (accessed July 4, 2024).

Burnard, K., & Bhamra, R. (2011). Organisational resilience: Development of a conceptual framework for organisational responses. *International Journal of Production Research, 49*, 5581–5599.

Burnard, K., Bhamra, R., & Tsinopoulos, C. (2018). Building organizational resilience: Four configurations. *IEEE Transactions on Engineering Management, 65*(3), 351–362.

Bushuyev, S., & Verenych, O. (2018). Organizational maturity and project: Program and portfolio success. In *Developing Organizational Maturity for Effective Project Management* (pp. 104–127). Hershey, PA: IGI Global.

Cabezas, H., Pawlowski, C. W., Mayer, A. L., & Hoagland, N. T. (2003). Sustainability: Ecological, social, economic, technological, and system perspectives. *Clean Technology and Environmental Policy, 5*, 167–180.

Cabezas, H., Pawlowski, C. W., Mayer, A. L., & Hoagland, N. T. (2005). Simulated experiments with complex sustainable systems: Ecology and technology. *Resources, Conservation and Recycling, 44*, 279–290.

Cabezas, H., Whitmore, H. W., Pawlowski, C. W., Mayer, A. L. (2007). On the sustainability of an integrated model system with industrial, ecological and macroeconomic components. *Resources, Conservation and Recycling, 50*, 122–129.

Caldara, D., & Iacoviello, M. (2022). Measuring geopolitical risk. *American Economic Review, 112*(4), 1194–1225.

Cempel, C. (2008). *Teoria i inżynieria systemów.* Radom: ITE.

Chen, J., Guo, X., Pan, H., & Zhong, S. (2021). What determines city's resilience against epidemic outbreak: Evidence from China's COVID-19 experience. *Sustainable Cities and Society, 70*, 102892.

Chen, Y., Chen, H., Gorkhali, A., Lu, Y., Ma, Y., & Li, L. (2016). Big data analytics and big data science: A survey. *Journal of Management Analytics, 3*(1), 1–42.

Ciasullo, M. V., Douglas, A., Romeo, E., & Capolupo, N. (2024). Lean Six Sigma and quality performance in Italian public and private hospitals: A gender perspective. *International Journal of Quality & Reliability Management, 41*(3), 964–989.

Clemente-Suárez, V. J., Navarro-Jiménez, E., Moreno-Luna, L., Saavedra-Serrano, M. C., Jimenez, M., Simón, J. A., & Tornero-Aguilera, J. F. (2021). The impact of the COVID-19 pandemic on social, health, and economy. *Sustainability, 13*(11), 6314.

Clohessy, T., & Acton, T. (2019). Investigating the influence of organizational factors on blockchain adoption: An innovation theory perspective. *Industrial Management & Data Systems, 119*(7), 1457–1491.

Coelho, P., Bessa, C., Landeck, J., & Silva, C. (2023). Industry 5.0: The arising of a concept. *Procedia Computer Science, 217*, 1137–1144.

Collins, D. J., & Montgomery, C. A. (1995). Competing on resources: Strategy in the 1990's. *Harvard Business Review, 73*, 110–128.

Correia, E., Carvalho, H., Azevedo, S. G., & Govindan, K. (2017). Maturity models in supply chain sustainability: A systematic literature review. *Sustainability, 9*, 64.

Correia, E., Garrido-Azevedo, S., & Carvalho, H. (2023). Supply chain sustainability: A model to assess the maturity level. *Systems, 11*(2), 98. https://doi.org/10.3390/systems11020098

Craigen, D., Diakun-Thibault, N., & Purse, R. (2014). Defining cybersecurity. *Technology Innovation Management Review, 4*(10), 13–21.

Crosby, P. (1979). *Quality is Free.* New York: McGraw-Hill.

Cuenca, L., Boza, A., Alemany, M. M. E., & Trienekens, J. J. M. (2013). Structural elements of coordination mechanisms in collaborative planning processes and their assessment through maturity models: Application to a ceramic tile company. *Computers in Industry, 66*, 898–911.

De Boer, F. G., Müller, C. J., & ten Caten, C. S. (2015). Assessment model for organizational business process maturity with a focus on BPM governance practices. *Business Process Management Journal, 21*(4), 908–927.

de Wit, B., & Meyer, R. (2007). *Synteza strategii.* Warszawa: PWE.

DeCarolis, J., Daly, H., Dodds, P., Keppo, I., Li, F., McDowall, W., ... Zeyringer, M. (2017). Formalizing best practice for energy system optimization modelling. *Applied Energy, 194*, 184–198.

DesJardine, M., Bansal, P., & Yang, Y. (2019). Bouncing back: Building resilience through social and environmental practices in the context of the 2008 global financial crisis. *Journal of Management, 45*(4), 1434–1460.

Dobrowolska, A. (2013). *Modele oceny dojrzałości zarządzania procesami biznesowymi.* Wrocław: Uwarunkowania dojrzałości organizacji w obszarze zarządzania i technologii.

Doguc, O. (2021). Applications of robotic process automation in finance and accounting. *Beykent Üniversitesi Fen ve Mühendislik Bilimleri Dergisi, 14*(1), 51–59.

Douglas, S., & Haley, G. (2024). Connecting organizational learning strategies to organizational resilience. *Development and Learning in Organizations: An International Journal, 38*(1), 12–15.

Dowling, T., & Pardoe, T. (2005). *TIMPA-Technology Insertion Metrics*. London: Ministry of Defence.

Duchek, S., Raetze, S., & Scheuch, I. (2020). The role of diversity in organizational resilience: A theoretical framework. *Business Research, 13*(2), 387–423.

Dunphy, D. C., Griffiths, A., & Benn, S. (2003). *Organizational Change for Corporate Sustainability: A Guide for Leaders and Change Agents for the Future*. London: Routledge.

Durand, T. (1997). Strategizing for innovation: competence analysis in assessing strategic change. In A. Heene & R. Sanchez (Eds.), *Competence-Based Strategic Management* (pp. 127–150). Chichester: John Wiley.

Dyllick, T., & Hockerts, K. (2002). Beyond the business case for corporate sustainability. *Business Strategy and the Environment, 11*, 130–141.

Dytwald, J. A. (1996). Zasoby przedsiębiorstwa. *Przegląd Organizacji, 3*, 23–26.

Eby, L. T., Adams, D. M., Russell, J. E., & Gaby, S. H. (2000). Perceptions of organizational readiness for change: Factors related to employees' reactions to the implementation of team-based selling. *Human Relations, 53*(3), 419–442.

Edgeman, R., & Eskildsen, J. (2014). Modeling and assessing sustainable enterprise excellence. *Business Strategy and the Environment, 23*(3), 173–187.

El Emam, K., & Madhavji, N. H. (1995). The reliability of measuring organizational maturity. *Software Process Improvement and Practice, 1*, 3–26.

Elkington, J. (1994). Towards the sustainable corporation: Win-win-win business strategies for sustainable development. *California Management Review, 36*(3), 90–100.

Elkington, J. (1997). *Cannibals with Forks: The Triple Bottom Line of 21st century Business*. Oxford: Capstone.

Farzin Abdehgah, E., Rastgooyan, S. B., & Khadivi, M. (2023). A bibliometric study of organizational storytelling/narrative research. *Journal of Design, Business & Society, 9*(2), 221–250.

Fiksel, J. (2003). Designing resilient, sustainable systems. *Environmental Science and Technology, 37*, 5330–5339.

Filimonau, V., & Coteau, D. A. (2019). De Food waste management in hospitality operations: A critical review. *Tourism Management, 71*, 234–245.

Fraser, P., & Gregory, M. (2002). The use of maturity models/grids as a tool in assessing product development capability. In *Proceedings of the Engineering Management Conference*, Cambridge, UK, 18–20 August 2002 (pp. 244–249).

Gajsek, B., Marolt, J., Rupnik, B., Lerher, T., & Sternad, M. (2019). Using maturity model and discrete-event simulation for Industry 4.0 implementation. *International Journal of Simulation Modelling, 18*(3), 488–499.

Gangwar, H., Date, H., & Ramaswamy, R. (2015). Understanding determinants of cloud computing adoption using an integrated TAM-TOE model. *Journal of Enterprise Information Management, 28*(1), 107–130.

Ghanem, M., & Ghaley, M. (2024). Building a framework for a resilience-based public private partnership. *Journal of Destination Marketing & Management, 31,* 100849.

Gierszewska, G., & Romanowska, M. (2014). *Analiza strategiczna przedsiębiorstwa.* Warszawa: PWE.

Gittell, J. H., Cameron, K., Lim, S., & Rivas, V. (2006). Relationships, layoffs, and organizational resilience: Airline industry responses to September 11. *The Journal of Applied Behavioral Science, 42*(3), 300–329.

Gobble, M. M. (2018). Digitalization, digitization, and innovation. *Research-Technology Management, 61*(4), 56–59.

Golinska, P., & Kuebler, F. (2014). The method for assessment of the sustainability maturity in remanufacturing companies. *Procedia CIRP, 15,* 201–206.

Golinska-Dawson, P., Werner-Lewandowska, K., Kolinska, K., & Kolinski, A. (2023). Impact of market drivers on the digital maturity of logistics processes in a supply chain. *Sustainability, 15*(4), 3120.

Gómez, J., Krammer, S. M., Pérez-Aradros, B., & Salazar, I. (2024). Resilience to the pandemic: The role of female management, multi-unit structure, and business model innovation. *Journal of Business Research, 172,* 114428.

Gościński, J. (1989). *Cykl życia organizacji.* Warszawa: PWE.

Gove, R., Sauser, B., & Ramirez-Marquez, J. (2008). Technology integration maturity metrics: Development of an integration readiness level. *International Journal of Technology Management, 9*(1), 17–46.

Graedel, T. E., & Klee, R. J. (2002). Getting serious about sustainability. *Environmental Science and Technology, 36,* 523–529.

Grandon, E. E., & Pearson, J. M. (2004). Electronic commerce adoption: An empirical study of small and medium US businesses. *Information & Management, 42*(1), 197–216.

Grant, R. M. (1991). *Contemporary Strategy Analysis: Concepts, Techniques, Application.* Cambridge, MA: Basil Blackwell.

Greiff, S., & Kyllonen, P. (2016). Contemporary assessment challenges: The measurement of 21st century skills. *Applied Measurement in Education, 29*(4), 243–244.

Grudzewski, W. M., Hejduk, I. K., Sankowska, A., & Wańtuchowicz, M. (2008). Cultural determinants of creating modern organisations–the role of trust. In *Working Conference on Virtual Enterprises* (pp. 323–332).

Hafeez, K., Zhang, Y., & Malak, N. (2002). Determining key capabilities of a firm using analytic hierarchy process. *International Journal of Production Economics, 76*(1), 39–51. https://doi.org/10.1016/S0925-5273(01)00141-4

Haffer, R. (2021). Supply chain performance measurement system of logistics service providers vs. supply chain performance: A conceptual framework. *European Research Studies, 24*(2B), 78–97.

Hall, R. (1992). The strategic analysis of intangible resources and capabilities to sustainable competitive advantage. *Strategic Management Journal, 13*, 135–144.

Hammer, M. (2007). The process audit. *Harvard Business Review, 85*(4), 111–123.

Hardjono, T., & Klein, P. D. (2004). Introduction on the European Corporate Sustainability Framework (ECSF). *Journal of Business Ethics, 55*, 99–113.

Haritas, I., & Das, A. (2023). Simple doable goals: A roadmap for multinationals to help achieve the UN's sustainable development goals. *Society and Business Review, 18*, 618–645.

Hart, S. L. (1995). A natural-resource-based view of the firm. *The Academy of Management Review, 20*(4), 986–1014.

Hart, S. L. (1997). Beyond Greening: Strategies for a sustainable world. *Harvard Business Review, 75*(1), 67–76.

Hart, S. L., & Milstein, M. B. (2003). Creating sustainable value. *Academy of Management Executive, 17*(2), 56–67.

Hassan, S. T., Wang, P., Khan, I., & Zhu, B. (2023). The impact of economic complexity, technology advancements, and nuclear energy consumption on the ecological footprint of the USA: Towards circular economy initiatives. *Gondwana Research, 113*, 237–246.

Haustein, S., Peters, I., Bar-Ilan, J., Priem, J., Shema, H., & Terliesner, J. (2014). Coverage and adoption of altmetrics sources in the bibliometric community. *Scientometrics, 101*, 1145–1163.

Helfrich, C. D., Blevins, D., Smith, J. L., Kelly, P. A., Hogan, T. P., Hagedorn, H., ... Sales, A. E. (2011). Predicting implementation from organizational readiness for change: A study protocol. *Implementation Science, 6*, 76.

Herbane, B. (2019). Rethinking organizational resilience and strategic renewal in SMEs. *Entrepreneurship & Regional Development, 31*(5–6), 476–495.

Herget, J. (2023). Development of corporate culture: Strategy generation. In *Shaping Corporate Culture: For Sustainable Business Success* (pp. 87–94). Berlin: Springer.

Hillson, D. (2003). Assessing organisational project management capability. *Journal of Facilities Management, 2*(3), 298–311. https://doi.org/10.1108/14725960410808276

Hillson, D. A., & Timerick, S. (2001). Project management benchmarking in theory and practice. In *Proceedings of the Effective Project Management 2001 Conference*.

Holden, M., Robinson, J., & Sheppard, S. (2016). From resilience to transformation via a regenerative sustainability development path. In Y. Yamagata, & H. Maruyama (Eds.), *Urban Resilience: A Transformative Approach* (pp. 295–319). Cham: Springer.

Humphrey, W. S. (1989). *Managing the Software Process*. New York: Addison-Wesley Longman.

Iacovou, C. L., Benbasat, I., & Dexter, A. S. (1995). Electronic data interchange and small organizations: Adoption and impact of technology. *MIS Quarterly, 19*, 465–485.

International Project Management Association (IPMA) (2019). https://old.ipma.pl/certyfikacja-organizacji-poprzez-ipma-delta%C2%AE (access: 4 July, 2024).

Ishak, A. W., & Williams, E. A. (2018). A dynamic model of organizational resilience: Adaptive and anchored approaches. *Corporate Communications: An International Journal, 23*(2), 180–196.

Ivert, L. K., & Jonsson, P. (2014). When should advanced planning and scheduling systems be used in sales and operations planning? *International Journal of Operations & Production Management, 34*(10), 1338–1362.

Jääskeläinen, A., Sillanpää, V., Helander, N., Leskelä, R. -L., Haavisto, I., Laasonen, V., & Torkki, P. (2022). Designing a maturity model for analyzing information and knowledge management in the public sector. *VINE Journal of Information and Knowledge Management Systems, 52*(1), 120–140.

Jamali, D. (2005). Changing management paradigms: Implications for educational institutions. *Journal of Management Development, 24*(2), 104–115.

Jämsä-Jounela, S. L. (2007). Future trends in process automation. *Annual Reviews in Control, 31*(2), 211–220.

Janasz, K., Janasz, W., Kozioł, K., & Szopik-Depczyńska, K. (2010).Wydawca: Koncepcje, metody, strategie DIFIN Rok wydania: 2010.

Järvinen, J., & Taiminen, H. (2016). Harnessing marketing automation for B2B content marketing. *Industrial Marketing Management, 54*, 164–175.

Jasiulewicz-Kaczmarek, M., & Prussak, W. (2012). Modele doskonałości w zarządzaniu jako- ścią. *Zarządzanie i Finanse*, nr 3/2012, 127–140.

Jennings, P. D., & Zandbergen, P. A. (1995). Ecologically sustainable organizations: An institutional approach. *Academy of Management Review, 20*(4), 1015–1052.

João Batista Sarmiento dos Santos-Neto & Ana Paula Cabral Seixas Costa (2019). Enterprise maturity models: a systematic literature review, *Enterprise Information Systems, 13(2)*, 1-51. https://doi:10.1080/17517575.2019.1575986

Juchniewicz, M. (2016). Osiąganie doskonałości w realizacji projektów przy wykorzystaniu modeli dojrzałości projektowej [w:] M. Trocki, E. Bukłaha (red.), Zarządzanie projektami–wyzwania i wyniki badań, Oficyna Wydawnicza SGH, Warszawa (pp. 35–57).

Kalinowski, T. B. (2012). Koncepcja oceny dojrzałości procesów logistycznych. *Zeszyty NaukoweUniwersytetu Ekonomicznego w Poznaniu, 224*, 37–47.

Kantur, D., & İşeri-Say, A. (2012). Organizational resilience: A conceptual integrative framework. *Journal of Management & Organization, 18*(6), 762–773.

Kazakovs, M., Verdina, A., & Arhipova, I. (2015). Automation of human resources development planning. *Procedia Computer Science, 77*, 234–239.

Khan, H., Ozkan, K. S., Deligonul, S., & Cavusgil, E. (2024). Redefining the organizational resilience construct using a frame based methodology: A new perspective from the ecology based approach. *Journal of Business Research, 172*, 114397.

Kim, H. L., & Hyun, S. S. (2024). Paradoxical effects of tourism ethnocentrism on domestic tourism: The moderating effect of pandemic anxiety travel. *International Journal of Tourism Research, 26*(1), e2628.

Kim, J., Song, H., & Luo, W. (2016). Broadening the understanding of social presence: Implications and contributions to the mediated communication and online education. *Computers in Human Behavior, 65*, 672–679.

King, D. D., Newman, A., & Luthans, F. (2016). Not if, but when we need resilience in the workplace. *Journal of Organizational Behavior, 37*(5), 782–786

Klasik, A. (Ed.). (1993). *Planowanie strategiczne.* Warszawa: PWE.

Klenner, P., Hüsig, S., & Dowling, M. (2013). Ex-ante evaluation of disruptive susceptibility in established value networks—When are markets ready for disruptive innovations? *Research Policy, 42*(4), 914–927.

Klimko, G. (2001, November). Knowledge management and maturity models: Building common understanding. In *Proceedings of the 2nd European Conference on Knowledge Management* (Vol. 2, pp. 269–278). Bled, Slovenia.

Kłos, Z. (2013). O niektórych modelach dojrzałości organizacji. In E. Skrzypek (Ed.), *Dojrzałość organizacji—aspekty jakościowe* (pp. 23–24). Lublin: Uniwersytet Marii Curic-Skłodowskiej w Lublinie.

Kober, B. J., & Sauser, B. (2008). A case study in implementing a system maturity metric. In *29th American Society of Engineering Management Conference* (pp. 555–563). New York: West Point.

Korber, S., & McNaughton, R. B. (2018). Resilience and entrepreneurship: A systematic literature review. *International Journal of Entrepreneurial Behavior & Research, 24*(7), 1129–1154.

Koronis, E., & Ponis, S. (2018). Better than before: The resilient organization in crisis mode. *Journal of Business Strategy, 39*(1), 32–42.

Kosieradzka, A. (2016). Modele dojrzałości jako narzędzie stymulowania zrównoważonego rozwoju organizacji. In J. Ejdys (Ed.), *Społeczna odpowiedzialność i zrównoważo- ny rozwój w naukach o zarządzaniu* (pp. 283–296). Toruń: TNOiK Dom Organizatora.

Kotler, P., & Armstrong, G. (2011). *Principles of Marketing* (14th ed.). Upper Saddle River, NJ: Prentice Hall.

Kotler, P., & Caslione, J. A. (2009). *Chaotics: The Business of Managing and Marketing in the Age of Turbulence.* New York: Amacom.

Kou, C., Meng, D., & Yang, X. (2024). Construction and application of economic resilience evaluation model for megacities. *PLoS One, 19*(5), e0301840.

Krishnan, V., & Gupta, S. (2001). Appropriateness and impact of platform-based product development. *Management Science, 47*(1), 52–68.

Krupa, M. (1999). *W poszukiwaniu doskonałości organizacyjnej.* Kluczbork: Antykwa Kraków.

Krupski, R. (2010). Kontekst chaosu w planowaniu strategicznym. *Przegląd Organizacji,* (3), 6–8.

Krupski, R. (2011). *Orientacja zasobowa w badaniach empirycznych. Identyfikacja horyzontu planowania rynkowych i zasobowych wielkości strategicznych.* Wałbrzych: Wałbrzyska Szkoła Zarządzania i Przedsiębiorczości.

Krupski, R. (2013). Rodzaje okazji w teorii i w praktyce zarządzania. *Prace Naukowe Wałbrzyskiej Wyższej Szkoły Zarządzania i Przedsiębiorczości, 21*(1), 5–16.

Kuc, B. R. (1999). *Zarządzanie doskonałe.* Warszawa: Publishing House Oskar-Master of Biznes.

Kumar, V., Srivastava, J., & Lazarevic, A. (Eds.). (2005). *Managing Cyber Threats: Issues, Approaches, and Challenges.* Springer Science & Business Media.

Kunasz, M. (2006). Zasoby przedsiębiorstwa w ekonomii. *Gospodarka Narodowa*, nr 10/2006, 33–48.

Kwon, J., & Johnson, M. E. (2013). Security practices and regulatory compliance in the healthcare industry. *Journal of the American Medical Informatics Association, 20*(1), 44–51.

Lahrmann, G., Marx, F., Winter, R., & Wortmann, F. (2011, January). Business intelligence maturity: Development and evaluation of a theoretical model. In *2011 44th Hawaii International Conference on System Sciences* (pp. 1–10). IEEE.

Lee, C. P., & Shim, J. P. (2007). An exploratory study of radio frequency identification (RFID) adoption in the healthcare industry. *European Journal of Information Systems, 16*, 712–724.

Lee, N. R., & Kotler, P. (2011). *Social Marketing: Influencing Behaviors for Good*. Los Angeles, CA: Sage.

Lengnick-Hall, C. A., Beck, T. E., & Lengnick-Hall, M. L. (2011). Developing a capacity for organizational resilience through strategic human resource management. *Human Resource Management Review, 21*(3), 243–255.

Lewandowski, M. (2016). Designing the business models for circular economy— Towards the conceptual framework. *Sustainability, 8*(1), 43.

Li, X., & Lin, H. (2024). How to leverage flexibility-oriented HRM systems to build organizational resilience in the digital era: The mediating role of intellectual capital. *Journal of Intellectual Capital, 25*(1), 1–22.

Lin, C.-T. (2003). Agility index in supply chain. *International Journal of Production Economics, 100*(2), 285–299.

Lin, W. L. (2023). Corporate social responsibility and irresponsibility: Effects on supply chain performance in the automotive industry under environmental turbulence. *Journal of Cleaner Production, 428*, 139033.

Lindgreen, A., & Swaen, V. (2010). Corporate social responsibility. *International Journal of Management Reviews, 12*(1), 1–7.

Lindström, C. W. J., Maleki Vishkaei, B., & De Giovanni, P. (2023). Subscription-based business models in the context of tech firms: Theory and applications. *International Journal of Industrial Engineering and Operations Management, 3*, 1–19.

Linnenluecke, M. K., & Griffiths, A. (2012). Assessing organizational resilience to climate and weather extremes: Complexities and methodological pathways. *Climatic Change, 113*, 933–947.

Lokuge, S., Sedera, D., Grover, V., & Dongming, X. (2019). Organizational readiness for digital innovation: Development and empirical calibration of a construct. *Information & Management, 56*(3), 445–461.

Looy, A. V., Backer, M. D., & Poels, G. (2014). A conceptual framework and classification of capability areas for business process maturity. *Enterprise Information Systems, 8*(2), 188–224.

Lovins, L. H., Lovins, A. B., & Hawken, P. (1999). A roadmap for natural capitalism. *Harvard Business Review, 77*(5/6), 145–158.

Lumpkin, G. T., Hills, G. E., & Shrader, R. C. (2004). Opportunity recognition. In *Entrepreneurship: The Way Ahead* (pp. 73–90). Routledge.

Ma, T., & Liu, Y. (2024). Multiple paths to enhancing the resilience of project-based organizations from the perspective of CSR configuration: Evidence from the Chinese construction industry. *Engineering, Construction and Architectural Management, 31*(2), 835–865.

Machado, C. G., Lima, E. P., Costa, S. E. G., Angelis, J. J., & Mattioda, R. A. (2017). Framing maturity based on sustainable operations management principles. *International Journal of Production Economics, 190*, 3–21.

Mallak, L. (1998). Putting organizational resilience to work. *Industrial Management-Chicago then Atlanta, 40*, 8–13.

Mani, V.; Agrawal, R.; Sharma, V., 2015, Social sustainability practices in the supply chain of Indian manufacturing industries. Int. J. Logist. Res. Appl. 2015, 1, 211–233.

Mankins, J. C. (1995). *Technology Readiness Levels, White Paper, Advanced Concepts Office*. Office of Space Access and Technology, NASA. http://www.hq.nasa.gov/office/codeq/trl/trl.pdf (access: 27.02.2023).

Marchesnay, M. (1994). *Zarządzanie strategiczne. Geneza i rozwój*. Warszawa: PWE.

Marshall, J. D., & Toffel, M. W. (2005). Framing the elusive concept of sustainability: A sustainable hierarchy. *Environmental Science and Technology, 39*(3), 673–682.

Martusewicz, J., & Szumowski, W. (2018). Modele dojrzałości a modele doskonałości. Niezależ- ność czy współzależność na drodze do rozwoju organizacji. *Organizacja i Kierowanie, 1*, 63–78.

Mary George, N., Parida, V., Lahti, T., & Wincent, J. (2016). A systematic literature review of entrepreneurial opportunity recognition: Insights on influencing factors. *International Entrepreneurship and Management Journal, 12*, 309–350.

Masaaki, I. (1986). *Kaizen: The Key to Japan's Competitive Success*. New York: Random House.

Masłyk–Musiał, E. (2012). Badanie wartości Politechniki Warszawskiej w kontekście strategicznym. *Zarządzanie Zasobami Ludzkimi, 2*, 109–124.

Matejun, M. (2016). Dynamic capabilities and the development of small business resource potential. *International Proceedings of Economics Development and Research, 86*, 83–92.

Matejun, M., & Nowicki, M. (2013). Organizacja w otoczeniu - od analizy otoczenia do dyna- micznej lokalizacji. In A. Adamik (Ed.), *Nauka o organizacji. Ujęcie dynamiczne* (pp. 152–221). Warszawa: Oficyna a Wolters Kluwer Business.

Matejun, M., & Walecka, A. (Eds.). (2013). *Modern Entrepreneurship in Business Practice: Selected Issues* (p. 149). Lodz: Lodz University of Technology Press.

Matwiejczuk, R. (2014). Z badań nad oddziaływaniem kompetencji logistyki na tworzenie przewagi konkurencyjnej przedsiębiorstwa. Gospodarka Materiałowa i Logistyka.

Mazurkiewicz, G. (2011). Edukacja w czasach globalizacji: niespełniona obietnica likwidacji nierówności.

McClory, S., Read, M., & Labib, A. (2017). Conceptualising the lessons-learned process in project management: Towards a triple-loop learning framework. *International Journal of Project Management, 35*(7), 1322–1335.

McDonough, W., & Braungart, M. (2002). Design for the triple top line: New tools for sustainable commerce. *Corporate Environmental Strategy, 9*(3), 251–258.

McManus, S., Seville, E., Vargo, J., & Brunsdon, D. (2008). Facilitated process for improving organizational resilience. *Natural Hazards Review, 9*(2), 81–90.

Mehrtens, J., Cragg, P. B., & Mills, A. M. (2001). A model of Internet adoption by SMEs. *Information & Management, 39*(3), 165–176.

Melnyk, M. V., & Nikitin, Y. O. (2021). Possibilities of creation and implementation of open innovations at R&D organizations of the NAS of Ukraine. *Science and Innovation, 17*, 96–103.

Mihlecic, J. R., Crittenden, J. C., Small, M. J., Shonnard, D. R., Hokanson, D. R., Zhang, Q., Chen, H., Sorby, S. A., James, V. U., Sutherland, J. W., & Schnoor, J. L. (2003). Sustainability science and engineering: The emergence of a new metadiscipline. *Environmental Science and Technology, 37*, 5314–5324.

Miller, D., & Shamsie, J. (1996). The resource-based view of the firm in two environments: The Hollywood film studios from 1936 to 1965. *Academy of Management Journal, 39*(3), 519–543.

Mittal, S., Khan, M. A., Romero, D., & Wuest, T. (2018). A critical review of smart manufacturing & Industry 4.0 maturity models: Implications for small and medium-sized enterprises (SMEs). *Journal of Manufacturing Systems, 49*, 194–214.

Molla, A. (2009). Organizational motivations for Green IT: Exploring Green IT matrix and motivation models. In *Pacific Asia Conference on Information Systems (PACIS) PACIS 2009 Proceedings* (p. 13).

Moreno-Monsalve, N., & Delgado-Ortiz, S. (2020). Knowledge management and its relationship with organizational maturity processes: An approach on project management. In *Handbook of Research on International Business and Models for Global Purpose-Driven Companies* (pp. 276–288).

Morisse, M., & Prigge, C. (2017). Design of a business resilience model for Industry 4.0 manufacturers. https://core.ac.uk/download/pdf/301371962.pdf

Motwani, J., Subramanian, R., & Gopalakrishna, P. (2005). Critical factors for successful ERP implementation: Exploratory findings from four case studies. *Computers in Industry, 56*(6), 529–544. https://doi.org/10.1016/j.compind.2005.02.005

Mukhopadhyay, S. C., & Suryadevara, N. K. (2014). *Internet of Things: Challenges and Opportunities*. Berlin: Springer.

Munir, M., Jajja, M. S. S., Chatha, K. A., & Farooq, S. (2020). Supply chain risk management and operational performance: The enabling role of supply chain integration. *International Journal of Production Economics, 227*, 107667.

Najm, N. A., & Ali, W. W. (2024). Organizational readiness and innovation in the Jordanian telecommunication companies. *International Journal of Productivity and Performance Management, 73*(1), 242–269.

Nick, G., Kovács, T., Kő, A., & Kádár, B. (2021). Industry 4.0 readiness in manufacturing: Company Compass 2.0, a renewed framework and solution for Industry 4.0 maturity assessment. *Procedia Manufacturing, 54*, 39–44.

Nitsche, B., Straube, F., & Wirth, M. (2021). Application areas and antecedents of automation in logistics and supply chain management: A conceptual framework. *Supply Chain Forum: An International Journal, 22*(3), 223–239.

Obłój, K. (2007). *Strategia organizacji.* Warszawa: PWE.

Olszewska, B. (Ed.). (2008). *Zarządzanie strategiczne, Przedsiębiorstwo na progu XXI wieku.* Wrocław: Uniwersytetu Ekonomicznego we Wrocławiu.

Ortiz-de-Mandojana, N., & Bansal, P. (2016). The long-term benefits of organizational resilience through sustainable business practices. *Strategic Management Journal, 37*(8), 1615 1631.

Pacchini, A. P. T., Lucato, W. C., Facchini, F., & Mummolo, G. (2019). The degree of readiness for the implementation of Industry 4.0. *Computers in Industry, 113*, 103125.

Pal, R., Torstensson, H., & Mattila, H. (2014). Antecedents of organizational resilience in economic crises-an empirical study of Swedish textile and clothing SMEs. *International Journal of Production Economics, 147*, 410–428.

Paschek, D., Luminosu, C. T., & Ocakci, E. (2022). Industry 5.0 challenges and perspectives for manufacturing systems in the society 5.0. In *Advances in Sustainability Science and Technology Sustainability and Innovation in Manufacturing Enterprises* (pp. 17–63). Singapore: Springer.

Patriarca, R., Bergström, J., Di Gravio, G., & Costantino, F. (2018). Resilience engineering: Current status of the research and future challenges. *Safety Science, 102*, 79–100.

Paulk, M. C., Curtis, B., Chrissis, M. B., & Weber, C. V. (1993). Capability maturity model, version 1.1. *IEEE Software, 10*(4), 18–27.

Pennypacker, J. S., & Grant, K. P. (2002). Project management maturity: An industry-wide assessment. In *Paper presented at PMI® Research Conference 2002: Frontiers of Project Management Research and Applications, Seattle, Washington.* Newtown Square, PA: Project Management Institute.

Penrose, E. (1959). *The Theory of the Growth of the Firm.* Oxford: Oxford University Press.

Perechuda, K., & Sobińska, M. (Eds.). (2008). *Scenariusze, dialogi i procesy zarządzania wiedzą: praca zbiorowa.* Centrum Doradztwa i Informacji Difin.

Peteraf, M. A. (1993). The cornerstones of competitive advantage: A resource-based view. *Strategic Management Journal, 14*, 179–191.

Peters, T. J., & Waterman, R. H. (1982). *In Search of Excellence.* New York: Harper and Row.

Piegat, A. (2013). *Fuzzy Modeling and Control* (Vol. 69). Heidelberg: Physica-Verlag.

Pierścionek, Z. (2003). *Strategie konkurencji i rozwoju przedsiębiorstwa.* Warszawa: PWN.

Pietruszka-Ortyl, A. (2012). Szkice o paradygmatach wyłaniających się w naukach o zarzą- dzaniu. In B. Mikuła (Ed.), *Historia i perspektywy nauk o zarządzaniu. Księga pamiątkowa dla uczczenia jubileuszu 40-lecia pracy naukowo-dydaktycznej prof. zw. dra hab* (pp. 69–80). Kraków: Arkadiusza Potockiego, Fundacja Uniwersytetu Ekonomicznego w Krakowie.

Pigosso, D. C., Rozenfeld, H., & McAloone, T. C. (2013). Ecodesign maturity model: A management framework to support ecodesign implementation into manufacturing companies. *Journal of Cleaner Production, 59*, 160–173.

Pires, A. S., Andrade, J., Barbosa, S. O., & Araujo, C. (2021). Analysis of the level of maturity in knowledge management at the Santa Catarina State Transplant Center. In *Proceedings of the 30th International Conference of the International Association for Management of Technology, IAMOT 2021 - MOT for the World of the Future* (pp. 838–848).

Porter, M. E. (2005). Czym jest strategia. Harvard Business Review Polska, lipiec–sierpień (pp. 161–185).

Porter, M. E., & van der Linde, C. (1995). Green and competitive. *Harvard Business Review, 73,* 120–134.

Porter, M. E., & van der Linde, C. (1997). Medio ambiente y competitividad. *Oikos,* (10), 61–75.

Prayag, G., Muskat, B., & Dassanayake, C. (2024). Leading for resilience: Fostering employee and organizational resilience in tourism firms. *Journal of Travel Research, 63*(3), 659-680.

Raikes, J., Smith, T. F., Powell, N., Thomsen, D. C., Friman, E., Kronlid, D., & Sidle, R. (2022). Crisis management: Regional approaches to geopolitical crises and natural hazards. *Geographical Research, 60*(1), 168–178.

Raissi, N., & Hakeem, A. (2023). Aligning process-based knowledge management with competencies behaviour: Effects of ISO practices. *International Journal of Project Organisation and Management, 15*(2), 218–252.

Ramdani, B., Kawalek, P., & Lorenzo, O. (2009). Predicting SMEs' adoption of enterprise systems. *Journal of Enterprise Information Management, 22*(1/2), 10–24.

Resemann, M., & de Bruin, T. (2005). Towards a business process management maturity model. In W. F. Rajola, D. Avison, R. Winter, J. Becker, P. Ein-Dor, D. Bartmann et al. (Eds.), *ECIS 2005 Proceedings of the Thirteenth European Conference on Information Systems* (pp. 1–12). Verlag and the London School of Economics, CD-ROM.

Rokita, J. (2005). *Zarządzanie strategiczne. Tworzenie i utrzymywanie przewagi konkurencyjnej.* Warszawa: PWE.

Rokita, J. (2009). Dynamika zarządzania organizacjami. Prace Naukowe/Akademia Ekonomiczna w Katowicach.

Romanowska, M. (2007). Trwałe tendencje w zarządzaniu. *Organizacja i Kierowanie,* (1), 65–68.

Romanowska, M. (2012). Uwarunkowania odporności przedsiębiorstw na kryzys makroeko- nomiczny. Propozycja podejścia badawczego. In A. Barabasz & G. Bełz (Eds.), *Systemy i procesy zmian w zarządzaniu* (pp. 231–251). Wrocław: Uniwersytet Ekonomiczny we Wrocławiu.

Ruegg-Sturm, J. (1998). New systemic theory and intra-company changes. *Problems of Theory and Practice of Management, 5,* 106–111.

Rumelt, R. P. (1991). How much does industry matter?. *Strategic Management Journal, 12*(3), 167–185.

Rupik, K. (2011). Planowanie w turbulentnym otoczeniu. *Master of Business Administration, 4*(111), 37–47.

Rybak, M. (Ed.). (2003). *Kapitał ludzki a konkurencyjność przedsiębiorstw.* Warszawa: Poltext.

Saaty, T. L. (2004). Decision making—The analytic hierarchy and network processes (AHP/ANP). *Journal of Systems Science and Systems Engineering, 13*, 1–35.

Safari, A., Balicevac Al Ismail, V., Parast, M., Gölgeci, I., & Pokharel, S. (2024). Supply chain risk and resilience in startups,SMEs, and large enterprises: a systematic review and directions for research. International Journal of LogisticsManagement, 35(2). https://doi.org/10.1108/IJLM-10-2022-0422

Sajdak, M. (2010). Podejście zasobowe jako podstawa wyborów strategicznych. *Zeszyty Naukowe Uniwersytetu Ekonomicznego w Poznaniu, 134*, 46–61.

Sajdak, M. (2013). The influence of agility on creating a competitive advantage and on company performance. In *2013 IMRA & RIT-ACMT International Conference* in-person 16th to 17th May 2013, Zagreb.

Samanta, M., Virmani, N., Singh, R. K., Haque, S. -N., & Jamshed, M. (2023). Analysis of critical success factors for successful integration of lean six sigma and Industry 4.0 for organizational excellence. *The TQM Journal, 36*(1), https://doi.org/10.1108/TQM-07-2022-0215

Sanchez, R., & Heene, A. (1996). A systems view of the firm in competence-based competition. In R. Sanchez, A. Heene, & H. Thomas (Eds.), *Dynamics of Competence-Based Competition* (pp. 39–62). Oxford: Elsevier.

Sanchez, R., & Heene, A. (2004). *The New Strategic Management: Organization, Competition, and Competence.* New York: John Wiley.

Santos, Â. R. S., Melo, R. M., Clemente, T. R. N., & Machado Santos, S. (2022). Integrated management system: methodology for maturity assessment in food industries, *Benchmarking, 29*(6), 1757–1780.

Santos-Neto, J. B. S. D., & Costa, A. P. C. S. (2019). Enterprise maturity models: A systematic literature review. *Enterprise Information Systems, 13*(5), 719–769.

Sarker, I. H. (2023). Machine learning for intelligent data analysis and automation in cybersecurity: Current and future prospects. *Annals of Data Science, 10*(6), 1473–1498.

Sauser, B. J., Ramirez-Marquez, J. E., Henry, D., & Donald DiMarzio, D. (2008). A system maturity index for the systems engineering life cycle. *International Journal of Industrial and Systems Engineering, 3*(6), 673–691. https://doi.org/10.1504/IJISE.2008.02068

Sauser, B., Ramirez-Marquez, J. E., Magnaye, R., & Tan, W. (2008). A systems approach to expanding the technology readiness level within defense acquisition. *International Journal of Defense Acquisition Management*, 1–48.

Sauser, B., Verma, D., Ramirez-Marquez, J., & Gove, R. (2006, April). From TRL to SRL: The concept of systems readiness levels. In *Conference on Systems Engineering Research* (Vol. 5, No. 0002, pp. 5–7). Los Angeles, CA: Stevens Institute of Technology.

Say, J. B. (2001). *A Treatise on Political Economy; Or the Production Distribution and Consumption of Wealth* (Translated from the fourth edition of the French). Kitchener: Batoche Books.

Scharfman, M. P., & Dean, Jr., J. W. (1991). Conceptualizing and measuring the organizational environment: A multidimensional approach. *Journal of Management, 17*(4): 681–700.

Schumacher, A., Erol, S., & Sihn, W. (2016). A maturity model for assessing Industry 4.0 readiness and maturity of manufacturing enterprises. *Procedia CIRP, 52*, 161–166.

Schumpeter, J. A. (1954). Joseph A. Schumpeter. Mohr.

SEI (2009). *SEI Annual Report 2008*. Stockholm, Sweden: SEI.

Seidel, A., Saurin, T. A., Marodin, G. A., & Ribeiro, J. L. D. (2017). Lean leadership competencies: A multi-method study. *Management Decision, 55*(10), 2163–2180.

Shahzad, K., Zhang, Q., Zafar, A. U., Shahzad, M. F., & Liu, W. (2024). Consumers' concerns and the role of blockchain technology in mobile food delivery applications. *Journal of Destination Marketing & Management, 32*, 100877. https://doi.org/10.1016/j.jdmm.2024.100877

Shahzad, U., Mohammed, K. S., Tiwari, S., Nakonieczny, J., & Nesterowicz, R. (2023). Connectedness between geopolitical risk, financial instability indices and precious metals markets: Novel findings from Russia Ukraine conflict perspective. *Resources Policy, 80*, 103190.

Shane, S. (2000). Prior knowledge and the discovery of entrepreneurial opportunities. *Organization Science, 11*(4), 448–469.

Shane, S., & Venkataraman, S. (2000). The promise of entrepreneurship as a field of research. *Academy of Management Review, 25*(1), 217–226.

Sharplin, A. D. (1985). Human resource planning: Low-cost strategies to improve worker's job security. *Journal of Business Strategy, 5*(3), 90–93.

Shaw, M. J., Solberg, J. J., & Woo, T. C. (1992). System integration in intelligent manufacturing: An introduction. *IIE Transactions, 24*(3), 2–6.

Shela, V., Ramayah, T., & Ahmad, N. H. (2024). Does organizational resilience matter? Fix it through improvisation! *Development and Learning in Organizations: An International Journal, 38*(1), 20–22.

Sincorá, L. A., Oliveira, M. P. V. D., Zanquetto-Filho, H., & Ladeira, M. B. (2018). Business analytics leveraging resilience in organizational processes. *RAUSP Management Journal, 53*, 385–403.

Sisinni, E., Saifullah, A., Han, S., Jennehag, U., & Gidlund, M. (2018). Industrial internet of things: Challenges, opportunities, and directions. *IEEE Transactions on Industrial Informatics, 14*(11), 4724–4734.

Skrzypek, A. (2014). Dojrzałość organizacyjna i jej wpływ na doskonalenie zarządzania przedsiębiorstwem. *Problemy Jakości, 46*(11), 8–12.

Skrzypek, A. (2022). Dojrzłość organizacji – źrodła, uwarunkowania i konsekwencje. *Nowe tendencje w zarządzaniu, 2*, 51–74.

Skrzypek, E. (2013). *Dojrzałość jakościowa a wyniki przedsiębiorstw zorientowa-nych projakościowo*. Warszawa: Difin.

Smite, D., & Moe, N. B. (2023). The role of responsiveness to change in large onboarding campaigns In *International Conference on Agile Software Development* (pp. 132–148). Cham: Springer Nature Switzerland.

Smite, D., Moe, N. B., Hildrum, J., Gonzalez-Huerta, J., & Mendez, D. (2023). Work-from-home is here to stay: Call for flexibility in post-pandemic work policies. *Journal of Systems and Software, 195*, 111552.

Somers, S. (2009). Measuring resilience potential: An adaptive strategy for organizational crisis planning. *Journal of Contingencies and Crisis Management,
17*(1), 12–23.

Sorychta-Wojsczyk, B. (2018). Analiza dojrzałości projektowej w jednost-
kach samorządu terytorialnego–studium literaturowe. Zeszyty Naukowe.
Organizacja i Zarządzanie/Politechnika Śląska

Srai, J. S., Alinaghian, L. S., & Kirkwood, D. A. (2013). Understanding sustainable
supply network capabilities of multinationals: A capability maturity model
approach. *Proceedings of the Institution of Mechanical Engineers, Part B:
Journal of Engineering Manufacture, 227*(4), 595–615.

Stachowiak, A. (2019). *Od organizacji stabilnej do odpornej: model dojrzałości organizacyjnej zwinnego przedsiębiorstwa.* Poznań: Wyd. Politechniki Poznańskiej.

Stachowiak, A., & Oleśków-Szłapka, J. (2018). Agility capability maturity framework. *Procedia Manufacturing, 17*, 603–610. https://doi.org/10.1016/j.
promfg.2018.10.102.

Stachowiak, A., & Pawłyszyn, I. (2021). From fragility through agility to resilience:
The role of sustainable improvement in increasing organizational maturity.
Sustainability, 13(9), 4991.

Stachowiak, Z., & Stachowiak, B. (2015). *Ekonomia gospodarki rynkowej Ujęcie
instytucjonalne.* Warszawa: Akademia Obrony Narodowej.

Staniec, I. (2017). Turbulentność otoczenia a źródła pozyskiwania technologii.
Handel Wewnętrzny, 3(368), 72–80 (tom II).

Stankiewicz, D. (2012). Zarządzanie różnorodnością jako zintegrowany model
biznesowy. *Przedsiębiorczość i Zarządzanie, Studia z zarządzania
międzykulturowego, 13*, 57–69.

Stanton, E. A. (2012). The tragedy of maldistribution: Climate, sustainability, and
equity. *Sustainability, 4*(3), 394–411.

Stevenson, A. (Ed.). (2010). *Oxford Dictionary of English.* Oxford University Press.
https://doi.org/10.1093/acref/9780199571123.001.001

Stoner, J. A. F., & Wankel, C. (1997). *Kierowanie.* Warszawa: PWE.

Sulimowska-Formowicz, M. (2002). Nurt zasobowy w teorii firmy. *Gospodarka
Narodowa,* (5–6), 41–60.

Sull, D. (2009). How to thrive in turbulent markets. *Harvard Business Review,
87*(2), 78–88.

Sullivan-Taylor, B., & Branicki, L. (2011). Creating resilient SMEs: Why one size
might not fit all. *International Journal of Production Research, 49*(18),
5565–5579.

Sutherland, W., & Jarrahi, M. H. (2018). The sharing economy and digital platforms: A review and research agenda. *International Journal of Information
Management, 43*, 328–341.

Teece, D. J., Pisano, G., & Shuen, A. (1997). Dynamic capabilities and strategic
management. *Strategic Management Journal, 18*(7), 509–533.

Tekletsion, B. F., Gomes, J. F. D. S., & Tefera, B. (2024). Organizational resilience
as paradox management: A systematic review of the literature. *Journal of
Contingencies and Crisis Management, 32*(1), e12495.

Tetlay, A., & John, P. (2009). Determining the lines of system maturity, system readiness and capability readiness in the system development lifecycle. In *7th Annual Conference on Systems Engineering Research 2009 (CSER 2009)*.

Tierney, K. J. (2003). Conceptualizing and measuring organizational and community resilience: Lessons from the emergency response following the September 11, 2001 attack on the World Trade Center.

Tietenberg, T., & Lewis, L. (2008). *Environmental and Natural Resource Economics* (8th ed.). New York: Prentice Hall.

Tiwari, P., Miao, J., Wang, Z., Wu, Z., & Ning, X. (2024). A blockchain-enabled privacy-preserving authentication management protocol for Internet of Medical Things. *Expert Systems with Applications, 237*, 121329.

Toeffler, A. (1995). *Creating a New Civilization: The Politics of the Third Wave*. Turner Publishing.

Trzcieliński, S. (2011). *Agile Enterprise*. Poznan: Publishing House of the Poznan University of Technology (in Polish).

Trzcieliński, S. (2011). *Przedsiębiorstwo zwinne*. Poznań: Wydawnictwo Politechniki Poznańskiej.

Turner, R. K., & Pearce, D. W. (1990). *The Ethical Foundations of Sustainable Economic Development*. London: International Institute for Environment and Development.

Ucal, M., & Xydis, G. (2020). Multidirectional relationship between energy resources, climate changes and sustainable development: Technoeconomic analysis. *Sustainable Cities and Society, 60*, 102210.

Ullah, A., Anwar, S. M., Li, J., Nadeem, L., Mahmood, T., Rehman, A., & Saba, T. (2024). Smart cities: The role of Internet of Things and machine learning in realizing a data-centric smart environment. *Complex & Intelligent Systems, 10*(1), 1607–1637.

Unruh, G. C. (2008). The biosphere rules. *Harvard Business Review, 2*, 111–117.

Wach, K. (1998). Identyfikacja i strukturyzacja cech otoczenia przedsiębiorstwa. *Organizacja i Kierowanie, 1*(131), 57–72.

Weaver, P., Jansen, L., Van Grootveld, G., Van Spiegel, E., & Vergragt, P. (2017). *Sustainable Technology Development*. London: Routledge.

Wechsler, D. (1950). Cognitive, conative, and non-intellective intelligence. *American Psychologist, 5*(3), 78–83.

Weick, K. E. (1996). Drop your tools: An allegory for organizational studies. *Administrative Science Quarterly, 41*, 301–313.

Weiner, B. J. (2009). A theory of organizational readiness for change. *Implementation Science, 4*, 67. https://doi.org/10.1186/1748-5908-4-67

Weiner, B. J., Amick, H., & Lee, S. Y. D. (2008). Conceptualization and measurement of organizational readiness for change: A review of the literature in health services research and other fields. *Medical Care Research and Review, 65*(4), 379–436.

Wendler, R. (2012). The maturity of maturity model research: A systematic mapping study. *Information and Software Technology, 54*(12), 1317–1339.

Wernerfelt, B. (1984). A resource-based view of the firm. *Strategic Management Journal, 5*(2), 171–180.

Werner-Lewandowska, K. (2020). Logistics maturity in service enterprises – research results. In *Proceedings of the 35th International Business Information Management Association Conference (IBIMA), 1-2 April 2020 Seville, Spain Education Excellence and Innovation Management: A 2025 Vision to Sustain Economic Development during Global Challenges* (pp. 3619–3634).

Wicker, P., & Breuer, C. (2013). Understanding the importance of organizational resources to explain organizational problems: Evidence from nonprofit sport clubs in Germany. *VOLUNTAS: International Journal of Voluntary and Nonprofit Organizations, 24*, 461–484.

Wicker, P., Filo, K., & Cuskelly, G. (2013). Organizational resilience of community sport clubs impacted by natural disasters. *Journal of Sport Management, 27*(6), 510–525.

Williams, A., Kennedy, S., Philipp, F., & Whiteman, G. (2017). Systems thinking: A review of sustainability management research. *Journal of Cleaner Production, 148*, 866–881.

Win, M. Z., Conti, A., Mazuelas, S., Shen, Y., Gifford, W. M., Dardari, D., & Chiani, M. (2011). Network localization and navigation via cooperation. *IEEE Communications Magazine, 49*(5), 56–62.

Wong, A. Y., & Fong, T. P. W. (2011). Analysing interconnectivity among economies. *Emerging Markets Review, 12*(4), 432–442.

Wysokińska-Senkus, A. (2013). *Doskonalenie systemowego zarządzania w kontekście sustainability*. Warszawa: Difin.

Xu, X., Lu, Y., Vogel-Heuser, B., & Wang, L. (2021). Industry 4.0 and Industry 5.0-Inception, conception and perception. *Journal of manufacturing systems, 61*, 530–535.

Young, W., & Tilley, F. (2006). Can business move beyond efficiency? The shift toward effectiveness and equity in the corporate sustainability debate. *Business Strategy and the Environment, 15*, 402–415.

Zabłocka-Kluczka, A. (2012). Odporność organizacji na kryzys. *Prace Naukowe Uniwersytetu Ekonomicznego we Wrocławiu*, (276), 89–101.

Zardini, G., Lanzetti, N., Pavone, M., & Frazzoli, E. (2022). Analysis and control of autonomous mobility-on-demand systems. *Annual Review of Control, Robotics, and Autonomous Systems, 5*, 633–658.

Zaufal, B. (1987). *O potrzebach kodeksu ekorozwoju*, Aura nr 12, (pp. 27–15).

Zennyo, Y. (2020). Freemium competition among ad-sponsored platforms. *Information Economics and Policy, 50*, 100848.

Index

Note: **Bold** page numbers refer to tables and *italic* page numbers refer to figures.

Printed in the United States
by Baker & Taylor Publisher Services